UNIVERSITIES AND TH...

Universities and the Future of America

*This volume is an expansion of the
Sanford Lectures delivered by Derek Bok at
Duke University on March 23 and 24, 1988.
The lectures are sponsored by the
William R. Kenan, Jr., Charitable Trust
Endowment Fund in honor of Terry Sanford
and arranged by the Institute for Policy
Sciences and Public Affairs
of the University.*

Universities and the Future of America

DEREK BOK

Duke University Press   *Durham and London*   1990

CONTENTS

PREFACE

T his book grew out of the Terry Sanford Distinguished Lectures which I delivered at Duke University in the spring of 1988. These lectures in turn are the product of many years of thinking about what Harvard and other universities might do to help our country cope more effectively with a formidable array of problems. If my analysis seems critical, it is not out of any disrespect for universities. Quite the contrary. It is my high regard for these institutions that leads me to believe that they can do more, much more, to contribute to a society sorely in need of their help.

I am grateful to several people who took the trouble to read drafts of the manuscript at various stages in its development: Harvey Brooks, Malcolm Gillis, Patricia Graham and, most of all, my wife, Sissela. Many of their suggestions found their way into the final text; the errors that remain are not of their making. Let me also give thanks to my loyal colleagues, Florence Gaylin, Janie Cohen, David Alcocer, and especially to Rogeria Cunningham, who cheerfully typed and retyped more versions of this manuscript than either of us cares to remember.

INTRODUCTION

—

In September of 1936, Harvard University celebrated its 300th anniversary. Crowds of alumni listened to a long series of speeches by leading scholars, educators, and public figures including a brief address by one of Harvard's most renowned but still controversial graduates, Franklin Delano Roosevelt. Through intermittent rains, one speaker after another reflected on the aims of higher education and its accomplishments over three centuries. The thoughts expressed were elevating; the rhetoric often eloquent. Yet nowhere in this bounty of words was there any premonition of the vast social changes and global events that would soon alter America's role in the world and transform its universities into huge, complicated institutions of great importance to the society.

At the time of the tercentenary celebrations, American universities were still elite institutions; barely 5 percent of young people in this country even graduated from college. Academic scientists were active in research, but their work attracted little notice in the outside world and brought only a pittance in support each year from the federal government. Modern medicine was still in its infancy; doctors could diagnose a number of diseases and describe their probable course, but all too rarely did they have the knowledge or the means to cure their patients. Until the turn of the century, the great inventions that spurred the progress of industry owed less to university investigators than they did to inventors such as Thomas Edison, Alexander Graham Bell, and the Wright brothers. Even when the large chemical companies and other corporations came to rely more on scientific research, their laboratories looked primarily to Europe, not America, for new ideas.

The Growing Importance of Universities

This sheltered era of higher education, celebrated with such pomp in Harvard Yard, came quickly to a close with the attack on Pearl Harbor. World War II revolutionized the university's place in American society. By inventions such as napalm and the atomic bomb, academic scientists demonstrated the uses of their research in terrifyingly effective ways. Impressed by these accomplishments, President Truman heeded the advice of Vannevar Bush soon after the War and created what would rapidly become a huge, government-supported program of academic research. In doing so, Truman was persuaded that university science would become a key to military preeminence and increasing prosperity. At the same time, fearful that returning veterans would glut the job market, Congress enacted the GI Bill in 1944 and began the transformation of higher education from a set of institutions serving an elite to one with an open door for all who were able and willing to seek further learning.

Events since World War II have confirmed the importance of universities to our society. Academic investigators have increased their share of scientific papers in most fields of research, becoming the dominant source of new discovery in many fields important to the nation. Favored by massive funding from the National Institutes of Health, medical school faculties have made striking contributions to our understanding of disease, and biological discoveries in the past quarter century promise an

even greater harvest of medical advances during the next generation. Our national defense has come to depend on science-based
inventions such as the laser, fiber optics, the semiconductor, and
many more. Our economy relies increasingly on technological
innovations drawn from modern science, with entire industries
being spawned by discoveries in biogenetics, materials science,
pharmacology, telecommunications, and microelectronics.

The changing needs of our society have also vindicated the
decision to encourage young people to enroll in colleges and
universities. The progress of science has been accompanied by a
steady advance in the skills demanded by modern industry. For
the first time, according to a recent study by the Hudson Institute, a majority of all new jobs developed between now and the
year 2000 will require at least some postsecondary education.[1]
Educational requirements for the military services have likewise
risen markedly. These tendencies are bound to grow stronger in
the future. As an editorial in *Science* points out: "Education,
broadly defined, will play a pivotal role in the coming economic
transition. . . . The changes underway in the economy are
placing an unprecedented demand on the intellectual skills and
knowledge of American workers."[2]

Through these developments, we have come to recognize that
all advanced nations depend increasingly on three critical elements: new discoveries, highly trained personnel, and expert
knowledge. In America, universities are primarily responsible
for supplying two of these ingredients and are a major source for
the third. That is why observers ranging from Harvard sociolo-
gist Daniel Bell to editorial writers from the *Washington Post* have
described the modern university as the central institution in
postindustrial society.

Fortunately, America's system of higher education is widely
perceived as unusually successful. In a recent poll taken in Asia,
eight out of the top twelve universities rated as the most out-

standing in the world were located in the United States.[3] American scientists, most of them professors, have won a majority of the Nobel Prizes awarded since World War II. Our colleges and universities educate a greater proportion of young people than those of any other nation. Our institutions of higher learning offer unequalled diversity to fit the needs of a vast heterogeneous student population. With many hundreds of independent centers of initiative, both public and private, our system yields more educational innovation and experimentation than its counterparts overseas. Because of these accomplishments, America is now the nation of choice for foreigners everywhere who are fortunate enough to be able to study abroad; one-third of all such students come to universities in this country. By almost any measure, then, higher education in the United States has no peer. Unlike so many other fields of endeavor, its lead over Europe and Japan has not diminished but may have even increased over the past quarter century.

If universities are so important to society and if ours are so superior, one might have thought that America would be flourishing in comparison with other industrialized countries of the world. Yet this is plainly not the case. To be sure, our form of society, marked by political democracy and a free market system, does appear to be prevailing over state-controlled economies and authoritarian forms of government. Welcome as this is, however, it hardly marks the "end of history" as some authors have recently claimed. The long cold war between democratic capitalism and authoritarian communism is not the only contest in which America has been engaged. If freedom and market economies prevail, their triumph will merely bring into sharper focus the other great challenge facing industrialized nations: how to build a society that combines a healthy, growing economy with an adequate measure of security, opportunity, and well-being for all its citizens.

At present, we are faltering in both aspects of this enterprise. After decades of exceptional progress, our economy has not been performing as well as that of most industrialized democracies. Productivity, the fruit of scientific and technological progress, has increased in the United States by less than one-quarter of the rate in Japan and Germany since 1960 and has lagged behind almost all industrialized nations in the last fifteen years. Our share of many important markets has shrunk severely in the past two decades, and even our trade balance in research-intensive, high-technology manufacturing goods went from highly positive in the 1960s and 1970s to negative in the 1980s. Held back by sluggish growth, our standard of living, which stood far above the level of Western Europe and Japan in the 1950s, was barely holding its own by the mid-1980s.*

---

*In reaction to the clamor over our declining competitiveness, articles have begun to appear that cast our situation in a happier light. E.g., Samuel P. Huntington, "The U.S.—Decline or Renewal?" *Foreign Affairs* (Spring 1988). The authors point to the last several years of unbroken prosperity, the successful efforts of many of our major corporations to improve productivity, and the recent growth of American exports. A few commentators have used this evidence to question whether there is any valid reason for concern about the economic performance of the United States. A close look at the evidence, however, quickly casts doubt on such optimistic notions. True, *industrial* productivity has grown quite rapidly in the last seven years. But our *overall* productivity has risen by little more than 1 percent per year since 1979, considerably less than in Japan, West Germany, or France. Moreover, much of the recent gain in manufacturing has resulted not from technological progress but from factors, such as our recovery from the 1980–82 recession and the closing of obsolete plants, that are not sustainable in the future. As for the recent growth in exports, these results have only come about through a drastic devaluation of the dollar, and even this adjustment has not succeeded in reducing our trade deficit below $100 billion per year. All in all, therefore, the facts strongly suggest that we continue to have a serious problem that must be addressed if we are to avoid a steady erosion of our economic position in the world.

At the same time, many social problems are more severe in the United States than elsewhere. As our economic position in the world has deteriorated, we have climbed to the top, or near the top, of all advanced countries in the percentage of the population who live in poverty, commit violent crimes, become addicted to drugs, have illegitimate children in their teens, or suffer from functional illiteracy. In a group of twenty nations, according to the latest international surveys, our high school students outdistance almost all their counterparts, not in their proficiency but in the number of errors they commit in science, mathematics, and reading comprehension.[4] In short, we lead most industrial democracies in ignorance and in many of the pathologies of modern civilization while lagging behind in the rate of economic progress.

These grim statistics should be profoundly troubling to those who devote their lives to higher education. On the surface, at least, one might have expected that the excellent science in our universities would place us at the forefront in maintaining the technological progress required to advance a highly developed economy. One might have hoped that our world-famous schools of business administration could have helped more to keep our companies competitive with their counterparts in Europe and Japan. One might have thought that graduates of our outstanding professional schools, armed with the research of our social scientists, could have done more to help our government agencies and community organizations to reduce the incidence of poverty, illiteracy, and stunted opportunity. Since these results have not occurred, it is fair to ask whether our universities are doing all that they can and should to help America surmount the obstacles that threaten to sap our economic strength and blight the lives of millions of our people.

This question raises two separate issues. The first is whether universities, especially our research universities, are doing enough to meet the many challenges that affect our ability to maintain a growing, competitive economy while providing adequate security and opportunity for all our citizens. In other words, are these universities contributing as much as they can to help society enjoy efficient corporate management, technological progress, competent government, effective public schools, and the conquest of poverty with its attendant afflictions of crime, drug abuse, alcoholism, and illiteracy? The second issue is moral in nature and recognizes that the revitalization of our corporations, our government agencies, our schools, and our urban areas is ultimately dependent on the values of individual citizens. Since values are so decisive, are our universities doing enough to build in our society—especially among its most influential members and leaders—a stronger sense of civic responsibility, ethical awareness, and concern for the interests of others? By asking how higher education is responding to both of these large issues, I hope to shed light on the ultimate question of what our universities contribute to the progress of society and how they can contribute even more.*

In choosing this subject, I am aware that it rests on a premise that is not universally accepted. Although most people take for granted that universities should help society address important issues, there are some who sharply disagree and even feel that such efforts have led to higher education's disorientation and decline. Such critics look approvingly on earlier conceptions of the academy, like that of Cardinal Newman more than a century ago, who saw the university as a place detached from society,

---

*Based on two public lectures, this short book cannot purport to cover all or nearly all of the societal problems to which universities can contribute through research and education. In particular, I have not been able to take up the important subject of how universities can contribute to such international issues as threats to the environment, Third World development, lasting peace, or population growth.

uncontaminated by its worldly values, and undistracted by pursuits other than the search for greater knowledge and understanding.

What troubles these observers most profoundly is the tendency of the modern university to be an instrument for careerism or social change rather than a place to seek truth as an end in itself. In the words of Wilfred Cantwell Smith:

> Traditionally, and essentially, universities were what they were—and uncontrivedly had the allegiance and respect that they deserved to have—because they were in pursuit of a truth that is above us all. . . . The shift in recent times has been from a notion of truth that we serve, to a different notion of truth as something that serves us. . . . We manufacture knowledge as we manufacture cars, and with similar objectives: to increase our power, pleasure, or profit—or if we are altruistic, to offer it to others so that they may increase theirs.[5]

To critics of this persuasion, any attempt to consider questions such as how higher education can help a nation to alleviate poverty or become competitive will be simply one more in a long series of efforts to pervert universities by using them as instruments, rather than places where students and professors search for knowledge for its own sake.

There is much worth pondering in this point of view. Certainly, we will debase our academic institutions and the work they do if we think of them merely, or even primarily, as means rather than ends. Conceiving of universities chiefly in instrumental terms can weaken the conviction of the faculty about the intrinsic worth of learning, undermine its intellectual standards and values, and expose it to endless petty distractions and corruptions from the outside world.* In concentrating on imme-

*I will not take time here to consider in detail the flimsier arguments made by critics who assert that the worldly pursuits of the modern university caused

diate problems, students will risk losing the greatest benefit of liberal learning—"the invitation to disentangle oneself from the urgencies of the here and now and to listen to the conversation in which human beings forever seek to understand themselves."[6]

It is of the utmost importance, then, that universities preserve abundant opportunities, especially in the colleges and traditionally academic disciplines, for professors and students to engage in intellectual inquiry for its own sake. Even committed utilitarians should accept this view once they remember how much works of sheer intellect and scholarship can contribute over the long run. After all, in the perspective of centuries, it is not generals and presidents, nor the experts who advised them, but social critics, philosophers, and the purest of scientists who have left the most enduring mark on our civilization.

It would be a pity, however, if an insistence on pure learning and research were to drive out all concern for practical issues. Not only does society need the university's help to solve many of its problems; such problems can also help scholars to discern more basic questions and to acquire practical experience that casts new light on familiar issues. Besides, the division between pure and instrumental inquiry is much too sharp. It is possible to explore a subject out of a keen desire to understand it better *and* a

---

higher education to fall from some early "golden age" and helped bring about the demoralization of faculty members in the face of student protests in the late 1960s. Those who hark back to a golden age rarely specify when this favored period occurred. They advance no facts to demonstrate the existence of such an era and ignore the considerable evidence suggesting that student learning and faculty research are, overall, more robust today than at any time in the past. As for the demoralization of faculty members, those who ascribe this phenomenon to the practical activities of universities do not explain why the loss of nerve was greatest in the humanities, where worldly involvements were least widespread. Nor do they tell us why faculties experienced similar problems in continental Europe even though most universities there have been much less involved in responding to social needs.

belief that such understanding may be of use to humankind, just as it is possible to understand oneself more deeply even while learning to practice a profession. One would suppose, therefore, that the true mission of universities would be to nurture a healthy balance between applied intellectual pursuits and the search for truth and meaning for their own sake.

It is also important to remember that higher education has changed profoundly since the time of Cardinal Newman. Several of these changes cast serious doubt on the wisdom of holding universities aloof from the society around them. To begin with, universities have now developed strong professional schools that make up an integral part of the institution. The central purpose of all these schools is to prepare their students for specialized careers and to investigate problems that practitioners have to confront in their working lives. There would be no convincing justification for these facilities if they did not concern themselves primarily with questions of practical interest to their professions.

Since Cardinal Newman wrote, moreover, American colleges and universities have ceased to be small, cloistered institutions serving a tiny elite. Together they enroll over 12 million students and employ more than 700,000 faculty members. Would even Newman insist that *all* these professors concentrate on learning for its own sake? Only a very few intellects in every generation have the capacity to do original work of pure research and scholarship. To them great honor is due; they represent the finest flowering of civilization. But it would be silly and precious to insist that work of this kind is the only proper pursuit for all or even a large fraction of our huge professoriate.

The growth of higher education gives rise to yet another objection to Newman's thesis. With their elaborate research programs and huge enrollments, modern universities require large amounts of funding from the public in order to carry on their normal activities. Professors receive over $6 billion every year in R & D funds from the federal government. State legislatures appropriate more than $35 billion annually to public institutions of higher learning. Universities as we know them could not survive without this massive assistance. Yet how could faculties possibly expect to go on receiving such support from the nation's taxpayers without making efforts to respond to society's needs?

Beyond these pragmatic considerations lies a more humane and moral reason for asking higher education to help meet the important challenges of our society. In contrast to the world in which Newman lived, advanced training, specialized knowledge, and scientific discovery are now essential to solving many urgent problems facing our civilization—problems of disease and health, of the environment, of economic progress, of human survival. Universities may not have any special capacity to prescribe solutions for the nation's ills. But they are better equipped than any other institution to produce the knowledge needed to arrive at effective solutions and to prepare the highly educated people required to carry them out. Possessed of these special capabilities, higher education cannot turn its back on human needs that require the advanced preparation and research that universities are uniquely able to provide. On the contrary, the very circumstances that have caused these institutions to prosper and to attract such recognition and support have also thrust upon them a heavy responsibility. Serving society is only one of higher education's functions, but it is surely among the most important. At a time when the nation has its full share of difficulties, therefore, the question is not whether universities need to concern themselves with society's problems but whether they are discharging this responsibility as well as they should.

CHAPTER ONE

The Contributions of Academic Science
to Greater Competitiveness

S ince 1946, when Vannevar Bush submitted his famous report on national science policy, Americans have put great faith in the capacity of basic research to help us build a stronger, more prosperous, more secure society. As Harvey Brooks has observed: "The implicit message of the Bush report seemed to be that technology was essentially the application of leading edge science and that, if the country created and sustained a first-class science establishment based primarily in the universities, the generation of new technology for national security, economic growth, job creation, and social welfare would follow almost automatically without explicit attention to all the other complementary pieces of the innovation system."[1]

In keeping with this faith in science, some commentators have suggested that an important reason for our sluggish productivity and our competitive decline is that the federal government has failed to maintain our national research effort by supplying it with sufficient funds. There is evidence to support this view. From 1967 to 1987 the share of GNP that Washington devotes to research and development (R & D) dropped from 2.1 to 1.3 percent. Outlays for civilian purposes lagged much more than military R & D over this period, and nonmilitary research is far more important for our productivity. Although rising corporate expenditures have helped offset this trend, our leading competi-

tors now spend relatively more than the United States on civilian
R & D. Thus, all nonmilitary outlays total less than 2 percent of
GNP in America compared with almost 2.6 percent in Japan and
2.8 percent in West Germany.

It should be noted that government funds for university
research have not fallen very much as a percentage of GNP.
Nevertheless, particular aspects of academic science in America
have been especially hard-hit. For example, grants for research
facilities have dropped by a staggering 95 percent since the 1960s,
while the number of federal fellowships and traineeships has
dipped by more than 25 percent. These declines help to explain a
backlog in renovations needed for academic laboratories that
government commissions have estimated at ten to twenty billion
dollars and a shortage of American graduate students that has
led leading departments of engineering and computer science to
admit 50 percent or more of their Ph.D. candidates from abroad.

In the wake of these trends, many voices have been heard
stressing the importance of research to economic growth and
prosperity. According to the president of Carnegie-Mellon University, Richard Cyert: "It is clear that knowledge is the source of
economic power in the United States. The major factor that will
determine progress is the amount of funding available for research."[2] Erich Bloch, director of the National Science Foundation, echoes these sentiments: "Investment in science and engineering research has been the source of much of our economic
progress over the past four decades."[3] Bloch adds: "Investment
in the knowledge base is consequently a major instrument of
competition for all nations. The most important thing a nation
can do to assure its economic prosperity is to maintain its
position at the frontiers of knowledge by investing in science and
engineering research. . . ."[4]

National commissions headed by leading industrialists have
made the same point in stressing the need to strengthen the

research capacity of universities. According to a 1986 report by the White House Science Council:

> The health of U.S. society is uniquely coupled to that of universities. To a greater degree than in any other country this Nation looks to its universities both for new knowledge and for young trained minds prepared to use it effectively. But just at a time when much is expected of our universities, after more than a decade of retrenchment and belt-tightening, they find themselves with obsolete equipment, aging facilities, and growing shortages of faculty members and students in many important fields. . . . Our conclusion is clear: our universities today simply cannot respond to society's expectations for them or discharge their national responsibilities in research and education without substantially increased support.[5]

Politicians, mindful of what universities have done to spur high-tech industry in Silicon Valley, Route 128, and the Research Triangle often endorse this conclusion and echo the call for more federal funding for university-based research.

Will Strengthening Basic Research Improve Our Competitive Position?

Arguments of this kind sound convincing. Before we swallow them whole, however, there are some awkward questions we need to answer. If basic research is so important to economic progress and productivity, why did the United States become economically dominant many decades ago when little scientific research was being done in American universities, and why did we decline competitively during the last quarter century when our universities and their scientific accomplishments have led the world? Conversely, why is it that Japan has been forging ahead so spectacularly when its universities and the quality of their research have been distinctly inferior to ours?

Against the backdrop of history, these paradoxes do not seem so baffling. For centuries, nations that have excelled in scientific discovery have not managed to lead in technological innovation and economic growth. In the Middle Ages, for example, the liveliest centers of science were located in China and Islam, but the greatest economic and commercial growth occurred in Europe. In the nineteenth century, England pioneered the development of the steam engine even though the underlying scientific discoveries occurred on the Continent. Conversely, Germans developed the synthetic dye industry on the basis of a fundamental discovery made by a British organic chemist.

There is a reason for this historical pattern. Until the late nineteenth century, industrial innovation did not depend heavily on science. Technological advances had mainly to do with levers, pulleys, gears, and other devices that were the natural province of inventors and engineers rather than university scientists. Not until the nineteenth century was nearly over did the process of technological innovation begin to draw significantly on the invisible world of atoms, molecules, bacteria, genes, and electromagnetic waves that only scientists could manipulate and understand. In earlier periods, therefore, one can readily understand why success in scientific discovery did not guarantee equivalent success economically.

In the modern era, technological innovation and science have become more and more closely intertwined. Entire industries have developed out of scientific discoveries, and modern corporations will pay millions of dollars to establish collaborative relations with leading university laboratories. Nevertheless, the relationship between basic research and technological innovation is much more complicated than one might suppose. Technological progress depends on knowledge derived from advances in basic research, but it also depends on entrepreneurial skill, engineering talent, and many other factors as well. As a result, scientific achievement is only moderately correlated with technological progress.

There is another, more obvious reason why preeminence in basic research may not cause a nation to attain a comparable leadership in technology. Science respects no national boundaries. By its very nature, it depends on a free and broad dissemination of results that allows investigators everywhere to profit from the work of others and to contribute something new in their turn. With information exchanged so freely, it is relatively easy for business enterprises in one country to learn of basic discoveries made in another. By reading scientific journals, sending scientists to international meetings, monitoring patents and trade journals, and encouraging graduate students to study abroad, Japanese and European concerns can readily stay abreast of scientific advances in the United States and quickly put them to use for their own commercial advantage.

This process is not confined to foreign companies. In this era of global enterprise, even American firms may take scientific work performed in this country and use it to improve the productivity of plants located overseas. And so it is that scientific leadership in the United States can fail to result in commercial leadership at home even in the most sophisticated technological industries. That is why the first fallacy in considering how to keep America competitive is to suppose that greater funding for academic science can do much by itself to reverse our decline.

Should We Keep Academic Science from Foreign Competitors?

The conclusion just expressed seems puzzling. Surely, leadership in science must have great potential value to a highly advanced economy. Isn't there something we could do to extract more competitive advantage from our uniquely strong capability in basic research? For example, why can't we improve our competitive position by keeping foreign governments and companies from having such ready access to American science? After all, thousands of scientists come to this country to learn our latest methods and take them back for use in their native countries. Foreign companies support research in our universities, often at bargain-basement prices, in order to "open a window" on American science. Are there barriers we could erect that would slow the transfer of new knowledge abroad and thus put foreign firms at a greater disadvantage?

With such thoughts in mind, government officials have already begun to make efforts to stem the outflow of new scientific knowledge. Congressional committees have criticized universities for making research agreements with foreign firms that may help the latter to reap the fruits of government-funded research. A bill was recently introduced in Congress to authorize federal agencies to withhold commercially promising discoveries produced in government-owned laboratories. Foreign scientists have been barred from a few scientific meetings, such as the 1986 White House conference on superconductivity. The Reagan administration even made a few, largely unsuccessful attempts to apply export restrictions to scientific and technical information that was "sensitive" in nature though not classifiable as military secrets.

Occasional efforts to shield research from foreigners have also been made by American universities. Carnegie-Mellon, for example, has actually restricted the number of Japanese graduate students and refused to accept research grants from Japanese companies. According to the provost, Angel Jordan, "There is some concern that this would be a transfer of technology to Japan, which we should avoid."[6] Similar thoughts have also been expressed by the media. Thus, the *Washington Post* has openly questioned the practice of allowing foreign graduate students to be educated in our science departments for the low tuitions commonly charged to Americans. As Michael Schrage put it: "What kind of policy is it that subsidizes America's corporate rivals with millions of dollars of our vital research?"[7]

While these concerns are understandable, any serious effort to restrict the number of foreign students studying science in our universities would be self-defeating and wrong. It would be churlish for a country whose science was built on the contributions of scientists from abroad to refuse to educate promising foreigners seeking instruction in our universities. Moreover, in contrast to the situation only a generation ago, we graduate fewer engineers and scientists relative to our population than our principal industrial competitors, and experts predict substantial shortages in both fields before the century comes to an end. As a result, our foreign students are a critical source of strength, for over half of them elect to stay in this country, and their contribution to American science and engineering would be difficult to replace from domestic sources. Under these circumstances, discouraging such students would only result in injuring ourselves.

It would be equally shortsighted to try to restrict the flow of information to foreign companies by barring research agreements or attendance at scientific conferences. There are many ways for foreign firms to keep up with scientific developments in America—by reading scientific journals, attending conferences, hiring recent Ph.D.'s, or acquiring an interest in U.S. companies. As a practical matter, it would be impossible to block all these channels effectively enough to make much practical difference. If we somehow managed to do so, scientific progress would quickly suffer, since science depends heavily on open communication among colleagues working in the same or related fields. Moreover, efforts on our part to stop the flow of information would undoubtedly provoke retaliation abroad, thus impeding scientific discovery even further. In research just as in commerce, free trade is the best way to secure progress for all.

But doesn't it go too far when American universities sign contracts with foreign companies accepting research funds in exchange for exclusive rights to exploit discoveries resulting from work done under the agreement? Does this not result, as some Congressmen have claimed, in allowing foreign rivals to profit at our expense from academic talent and facilities developed with money supplied by American taxpayers? Such arguments have obvious political appeal. Still, they are not terribly convincing. For one thing, it is not easy to tell what country will benefit from agreements of this kind. Arrangements made with American companies may result in discoveries used to manufacture abroad, while foreign companies may apply the discoveries made in American universities to manufacture in the United States. Moreover, forbidding research agreements with foreign corporations will simply reduce the amount of research performed by our universities. This reduction in turn threatens to slow the rate of progress not only for foreign consumers but for our own as well. For all these reasons, the notion that we should try to give ourselves a commercial advantage by hiding our discoveries from foreign firms is shortsighted and represents the second major fallacy in thinking about the effects of research on our economic competitiveness.

Should We Encourage Closer University-Industry Cooperation?

Instead of trying to keep our competitors from learning about our scientific discoveries, many people have urged universities to work more closely with American corporations to speed the translation of scientific knowledge into technological innovations. Such suggestions have met with enthusiasm from almost every quarter. Government officials hope that closer cooperation will give our companies a needed technological advantage. Corporations are eager to gain new knowledge in burgeoning fields, such as biogenetics, where discoveries may quickly lead to profitable new products. Universities have been quick to capitalize on opportunities to earn royalty income from successful patents and to gain corporate research funds in exchange for the promise of exclusive licenses on any discoveries that result. Academic scientists too have jumped at the chance of acquiring new sources of research support while benefiting personally from opportunities to earn large consulting fees or even hold stock in newly created companies.

Despite this enthusiasm, the new methods of cooperation promise to be something of a mixed blessing. On the positive side, preliminary reports suggest that research arrangements with universities are yielding several times as many patents as the same amount of corporate money invested in other, more traditional forms of company research. On the other hand, contracts with industry create special dangers for the type of academic environment needed for basic research. Companies may insist on secrecy requirements to protect proprietary information. The lure of commercial success can induce talented faculty members to spend too much time starting a company or consulting with established firms, so that the quality of their basic research may begin to suffer. It is even possible that some professors will exploit their graduate students by persuading them to work on commercially valuable research rather than projects of greater academic value. Carried to excess, such practices could corrupt basic research and eventually weaken it significantly.

It is still too early to tell what the net effect of industry-university cooperation will be. The reports to date have not substantiated early fears that academic science will be corrupted. Nevertheless, universities are constantly pressed to accept questionable arrangements with industry. More and more companies are asking that research contracts include provisions prohibiting academic scientists funded by one company from collaborating with investigators funded by another. More and more universities are agreeing to stricter limits on the use and disclosure of proprietary information obtained from the firms that fund them. A few institutions have even agreed to clauses that require them to keep faculty members from speaking about their commercially funded research at academic meetings without first submitting their remarks to their industrial sponsors.

These hazards cast doubt on the wisdom of pressing too hard to increase the number of research contracts with industry. Moreover, whether or not universities succeed in adequately protecting their essential academic values, it is unlikely that agreements with domestic corporations will ever be sufficient to improve our competitive position appreciably. Even if corporate support for academic science grew to twice the levels achieved in the 1970s—and it is unlikely to do more than that—the funds received would still amount to less than 10 percent of total university research. Besides, as we have seen, foreign firms have also been quick to sign research agreements with American universities, and there is no sign yet that they will be prohibited from doing so in the future. Once again, therefore, it seems difficult to translate the special strength of our academic research into a unique advantage for American business. Despite the publicity resulting from efforts to collaborate more closely with industry, the notion that such links will do much to restore the preeminence of American business constitutes the third major fallacy in the national debate over competitiveness.

The Real Causes of Our Competitive Decline

There is a more basic reason for doubting whether efforts to improve university-industry collaboration or any other policy focused on scientific research can do a great deal to strengthen our competitive position. If one examines the reasons for the loss of our economic leadership over the past few decades, the principal factors do not seem to involve a weakness in generating new technology. Notwithstanding some evidence of recent decline, the United States still accounts for roughly half of all new patents issued. Moreover, there are abundant signs of creative vigor in exploiting innovative ideas commercially. We do not suffer from any lack of resourceful entrepreneurs, nor does there appear to be any shortage of venture capital to back promising new initiatives.

Most experts have concluded that the real problems of American competitiveness do not lie early in the product cycle at the stage of making inventions or even starting new companies. The trouble typically begins in later phases when products must be standardized and produced in large quantities at low prices and high quality.[8] As two informed observers, David Teece and Henry Ergas, recently pointed out: "The Japanese did not invent the color television, the videotape recorder, or the semiconductor. But they developed designs and manufacturing systems that created decisive competitive advantage."[9] In short, our failure to capitalize on our successful initiatives has little to do with science. Rather, the principal causes lie elsewhere.

To begin with, the level of savings in this country has been lower for decades than in other industrial nations, and the gap has been growing greater. From 1962–86, average net savings amounted to 7.5 percent of GNP in the United States compared with 14 percent in West Germany, 15 percent in France, and a whopping 20 percent in Japan. Because the pool of American capital available for investment has been so restricted, our rate of spending on manufacturing plant and equipment has been much lower than in other industrialized nations for the past quarter century. The resulting gap has been a major factor in the sluggish growth of productivity in America over the past quarter of a century.

In addition, poorly conceived and poorly executed public policies have hampered productivity and growth. Federal deficits in recent years have helped to keep the cost of capital higher in the United States than in other industrial countries (three times the rate in Japan), thus inhibiting the amount of investment. Cumbersome regulations administered in an adversarial manner in fields such as environmental protection, safety, and antitrust have added to costs unnecessarily. Confused, uncoordinated trade policies have set government agencies at cross-purposes and prevented us from developing clear objectives and priorities, thus putting us at a serious disadvantage in international negotiations. Political pressures have often forced the government to spend more time and energy protecting sagging industries than promoting new ones. Finally, our inability to build effective programs to retrain laid off workers has prolonged unemployment and increased the costs of shifting from outmoded industries to growing enterprises with a future.

American managers must also share the blame for our poor economic performance. They have often been parochial in their outlook, exhibiting less skill than business executives from other countries in understanding how to penetrate foreign markets and adjust to different cultures and traditions. More troubling still, many executives in the United States seem to have grown complacent during the postwar years of our industrial preeminence. As a result, attention to quality has suffered, as anyone can observe by reading *Consumer Reports* and comparing the evaluations of Japanese and American automobiles and other common products and appliances. Influenced by our tax laws, American firms have also been preoccupied too much with problems of finance and short-term profitability and have failed to be sufficiently adept at ways of using technology and engineering to improve products and cut costs aggressively. Finally, American executives have lagged behind the Japanese in understanding how to organize and motivate workers. Despite the exaggerated claims that are sometimes made for quality circles and bottom-up management, most experts agree that Japan's success in raising productivity has been due more to the way it manages its work force than to its skill in technological innovation. That is why Japanese firms have typically outperformed American companies even while using essentially the same process technology and similar product designs.

Further problems have resulted from the disappointing record of our public schools. As production methods change more rapidly, formal schooling becomes more important to productivity. Yet American students, especially in high school, lag behind their counterparts in most other industrialized countries. This tendency has been particularly marked in mathematics and science. According to a recent international survey involving students from thirteen advanced or industrializing countries, seventeen-year-olds in the United States ranked ninth in physics, eleventh in chemistry, and thirteenth in biology.[10] American students also ranked lower than students in almost all other industrialized nations in geometry, algebra, measurement and calculus.[11] Small wonder: more than 50 percent of all teachers of math and science are not even certified as qualified to teach these subjects.[12] With inadequate instruction and encouragement, too few high school graduates are well enough prepared to become engineers and scientists. More broadly, "the fact that nearly half of [all] 17-year-olds do not have mathematical skills beyond basic computation with whole numbers has serious implications. With such limited mathematical abilities, these students nearing graduation are unlikely to be able to match mathematical tools to the demands of various problem situations that permeate life and work."[13]

The United States also lags behind several other nations in the vocational training it provides for young people. For example, although higher proportions of American youth graduate from high school than do young people in Switzerland and Germany, these countries have much more successful vocational and apprenticeship programs. Overall, therefore, their labor force appears to be more skilled than ours, more prepared for the needs of the economy, more capable of learning on the job, and more adaptable to technological change.

Finally, even apart from the suffering it produces, the persistence of a huge underclass in America acts as a gigantic anchor to slow the pace of economic progress. With 27 million functional illiterates, 33 million people in poverty, and many millions addicted to drugs and alcohol, vast sums of money must be spent on programs of welfare, law enforcement, social work, and other services that do not add to productivity. Functional illiteracy costs the nation an estimated $25 billion each year;[14] problem drinking and drug addiction cost an additional $62 billion annually.[15] School dropouts will cost many billions or more for welfare and remedial training over their working lives. Furthermore, because of the chronic unemployment, the spread of drugs, and the disintegration of families that are endemic in many urban communities, millions of children grow up without the necessary family support to encourage them to apply themselves in school. In these ways, poverty and its related ills tend to perpetuate conditions that produce large numbers of unskilled, undisciplined, unmotivated workers.

Once these relationships are understood, the need to provide reasonable opportunity and economic security to all members of society cannot be viewed as an aim separate from or in conflict with the need for growth and rising productivity. In fact, both aims are highly interdependent. Without the increments of wealth that growth provides, our society is unlikely to provide the funds required to overcome poverty, inadequate schooling, and urban decay. Without attacking poverty, inadequate education, and the social blights that follow in their wake, we will find it increasingly hard to compete with nations fortunate enough not to experience these handicaps on a comparable scale.

Do We Need So Much Basic Research?

For these reasons, a serious effort to insure the competitiveness of our economy—and the welfare and opportunities of our entire population—must attend to all of the problems just described. Yet none of these problems is closely linked to basic scientific research, nor is any of them likely to be affected very much by discoveries made in a university laboratory. In view of this conclusion, one cannot avoid asking one final question. If our unique strength in fundamental research yields so few competitive advantages, is it worth devoting $11 billion a year of public funds to support the enterprise? In these deficit-ridden times, wouldn't we do better to emulate the Japanese by spending less on basic science and relying more on discoveries made abroad?

In fact, to try to save money in this way would be to succumb to the fourth and final fallacy in the public debate over competitiveness. The reasons are simple. By cutting back our basic scientific research effort and relying more on discoveries abroad, we would shift the contest of innovation to the arena where we are likely to fare least well against our foreign rivals. Some of our leading competitors, notably Japan, conduct much more of their scientific research in corporations where it is less accessible to foreign eyes than comparable work carried on in academic laboratories in this country. Moreover, our parochialism and lack of language skills make us less prepared than other industrial nations to compete successfully in ferreting out new discoveries abroad. Already, only half as many American scientists collaborate with foreign colleagues as in France, Germany, or England. It is not surprising, then, that the share of royalties and licensing fees for technology that American firms pay to foreign companies has not risen over the past fifteen years even though the share of patents awarded to foreign firms and the share of first-rate scientific work done abroad have both grown dramatically. The less American corporations can rely on our own scientific discoveries, therefore, the more they are likely to fall behind in translating new knowledge into successful goods and services and more efficient methods of production.

There are other considerations that also argue strongly against cutting back our basic scientific research effort. As previously mentioned, we are not now able to attract enough talented people into science and engineering to satisfy our military and civilian needs. The shortfall of Ph.D.'s in these fields is expected to grow to several thousand per year within a decade. In the face of these deficits, we depend increasingly on foreign students who flock to our universities for advanced degrees and often stay on in America indefinitely. Such students are attracted to this country by the excellence of research in our leading universities. If this excellence were eroded and able foreign students began to go elsewhere for their training, the quality and quantity of our own scientific personnel would soon begin to suffer, for there is little immediate prospect of making up the deficit by increasing the number of American students going into science.

Finally, our leadership in basic research is important for yet another reason. The progress we make in health care, manufacturing, and other important areas will ultimately be influenced by the rate of scientific discovery worldwide. In turn, the success of science globally is heavily affected by the progress of research in the United States. Despite a gradual erosion in our position over the past twenty years, our scientists still account for almost one-half of all scientific discoveries and over one-third of all the scientific papers published throughout the globe. Thus, major cuts in American science would slow the rate of discovery throughout the world and eventually threaten progress everywhere in many fields of activity vital to human welfare.

This trend would become even more serious if other nations chose to emulate our example and cut back their research in order to save money. The results would be unfortunate for everyone, since in the end, what matters most to a nation is not whether it is growing faster than other countries but how rapidly it is improving its standard of living (and the quality of its health care and its environment). After all, we would hardly gain from growing faster than the Japanese if our GNP were rising at less than 1 percent and they had stopped growing altogether. Over the long term, they progress in science matters because it is a significant factor in determining the rate of economic progress and hence the ultimate level of prosperity and well-being we achieve. It is also indispensable to the intensely human urge to discover more about ourselves and the world that we inhabit. For these reasons, far from cutting our basic science effort, we should strengthen it, as national commissions have urged, by providing sorely needed funds for facilities, equipment, and graduate fellowships.

In sum, the quality of our university research remains a monument to our civilization and a potent force for long-term progress everywhere. Any major deterioration of our scientific effort would ultimately lessen economic progress and put us at a greater disadvantage vis-à-vis other industrial nations. Yet the point remains that strengthening research is *not* an effective strategy, as some enthusiasts imply, for balancing our trade account or allowing American companies to maintain a decisive lead over foreign competitors. Nor does it appear that we can gain the competitive edge we seek by keeping our academic research from foreigners or by sharing it more quickly with our own corporations.

If we mean to improve our economic competitiveness—and,

more important, increase our rate of productivity growth—we must come to grips with other problems in our society. Spokesmen for higher education should make this clear in their public statements and congressional appearances. Otherwise, they will only awaken unrealistic expectations and eventually cause resentment and disillusionment. Worse yet, they will blind themselves to more substantial contributions that universities *can* make to attack the roots of America's economic problems.

CHAPTER TWO

Universities and the Search for a Better Society

O n close examination, the issue of competitiveness turns out to involve questions of quality and productivity that stem from problems reaching far beyond the strength of our scientific research or even the competence of our engineers and corporate executives. To a considerable degree, our economic travails are also an outgrowth of many of our greatest shortcomings as a nation—the defects of our public schools, the deficiencies of our government, the persistence of poverty and the related misfortunes of joblessness, drugs, illiteracy, crime, and disintegrating families. Though short-term measures may bring temporary relief to our competitive position, we are not likely to sustain satisfactory economic growth for very long unless we make progress in conquering these underlying problems. More important still, until we overcome these problems, we will not succeed in becoming a truly humane society that offers adequate opportunities and support for all its citizens.

The Role for Higher Education

There is little that higher education can do to solve these problems directly. Universities cannot increase the rate of savings, change the policies of corporate executives, alleviate poverty, or reform government policy. They cannot even improve the quality of the public schools. But this does not mean that higher education has no useful role to play in addressing such issues. Universities can contribute indirectly but significantly to almost all the efforts required to make our economy stronger and our society more humane.

Nowhere is this more apparent than in the field of management education. If corporate executives must work harder to increase productivity, improve the quality and design of their products, and expand their sales abroad, business schools can give an important place to all these subjects in their curricula, both for MBA students and for mid-career executives. In doing so, instructors can draw from a broad spectrum of research not only in economics and management but in engineering, international studies, psychology, and other fields to suggest better ways of organizing work and motivating employees, more effectivemanagement of technology and design, and more perceptive methods of analyzing foreign economies and cultures. To buttress these efforts, professors can extend their research beyond the more theoretical forms of inquiry to investigate the actual strategies and practices of successful corporations in America and other nations around the world.

In selective business schools, admissions officers may further recognize the challenges facing business today by giving preference to students possessing foreign experience and language skills or scientific and engineering backgrounds. By doing so, such schools will not only attract students with knowledge relevant to pressing corporate problems; they will induce larger numbers of undergraduates to acquire these competencies. In turn, faculties of arts and sciences can strengthen foreign language requirements for undergraduates and encourage students to take more courses on foreign countries and cultures. They can also build vigorous centers of international and area studies and urge them to develop closer contacts with their business schools.

Engineering faculties likewise have a part to play. They can work actively to recruit and retain able undergraduates. They can take pains not only to emphasize basic scientific principles but to devote more attention to production engineering and product design. They can join with business schools to develop courses on the management of technology. They can also strengthen programs of mid-career education and persuade their alumni in the corporate sector to make full use of these opportunities to prolong and renew their engineering careers.

Because rules, regulations, and litigation play such a pervasive role in our society, law schools have contributions to make both to the challenge of competitiveness and to the problems of poverty. With respect to competitiveness, law faculties can strive in their research not only to analyze legal doctrine and discuss legal theory but to conduct empirical studies of the burdens of regulation and dispute resolution on the conduct of business. Through their teaching and research, they can try to build a greater awareness of the costs of regulation and litigation and a greater understanding of ways to avoid disputes or to keep litigation and regulatory expenses to a minimum. As for the problems of poverty, law schools cannot only offer courses and mount research on legal problems of the poor; they can enlist students in programs that offer legal services to the indigent and use these programs as a means of conducting fieldwork to discover more efficient, effective ways of resolving disputes and otherwise meeting the legal needs of poor communities.

The field of public administration offers even greater opportunities. Since the Great Depression, it has been apparent that government is a major force in our society, touching almost every important corner of our lives. It has also become clear that the policy issues public officials confront are more difficult than those encountered by any other group of professionals in our society and that the task of administering huge public agencies offers more severe challenges than those experienced by any other group of administrators. Because the practice of government is so important and so complex, the country badly needs able, well-trained public officials. As a result, universities attuned to the needs of society can try to build schools of public administration of a quality comparable to that of the most successful professional faculties in the university. Such schools can move aggressively to attract able students, not only recent college graduates contemplating government careers but also established career officials and politicians in need of well-designed executive programs. With needed funds and encouragement from university leaders, public administration faculties can gradually develop strong curricula in policy analysis and administration while mounting vigorous research efforts to expand our knowledge of policy formation and public management.

Because of the vast importance of education and the manifest failures of our public school systems, it is also important that universities maintain strong faculties of education. Our nation must replace half of its 2.5 million teachers within a few years. Our public school students are in evident need of more effective, challenging forms of instruction. Faced with these needs, alert education faculties should make every effort to provide the best possible methods of teacher preparation and reach out aggressively for recruits of all ages who are interested in teaching careers. In addition, now that leadership has been shown to be so important to the performance of effective schools, education faculties have a real chance to develop strong programs to train principals and superintendents, following the successful examples of executive training pioneered by business schools. Because there is still so much that we do not know about education, faculties can also make a valuable contribution by maintaining active research programs to discover more effective methods of teaching and learning, to analyze the success and failure of policies and programs of school reform, and to create better methods of assessment and evaluation. Through efforts of this kind, education schools can serve the entire university as models of good instruction and centers of creative experimentation to improve teaching and learning.

Finally, there is much useful work to be done in the field of poverty and its related misfortunes. Although the War Against Poverty was not the failure it is often made out to be, its demise brought home the fact that we do not yet know enough about the poor, the homeless, the chronically unemployed, and the high school dropouts to mount a wholly effective effort to help such persons overcome their disadvantages. Yet the costs to society of trying to cope with these problems run to many billions of dollars each year; the costs in terms of human misery are beyond economic calculation. Hence, it is only fitting that universities contemplate programs of research on these subjects comparable to the large-scale efforts currently devoted to AIDS, cancer, and other major diseases. And it is likewise important to mount strong educational programs to prepare the social workers and human services personnel who will be required to carry out government programs in poor communities.

In describing these possibilities, I do not claim that pursuing them will necessarily make American business more competitive, improve public policy, or overcome the problems of our urban ghettos. Knowing more about poverty does not guarantee that wiser legislation will be enacted, nor do better training programs for government officials and schoolteachers mean that graduates will use their knowledge to the best advantage. Political pressures, financial difficulties, self-interest, and other practical obstacles will often block the way. Still, the fact remains that our economy and our society are not likely to improve significantly *without* the benefit of greater knowledge than we currently possess and larger numbers of well-prepared teachers, business executives, engineers, and public servants. In this sense, universities have an essential contribution to make in improving our society along with corporations, government agencies, and other major institutions.

The Response

Faced with this array of important possibilities, what have universities done to respond? Surprisingly little. To understand how disappointing the record has been, let us look briefly at higher education's response to each of the opportunities just described.

Despite our growing involvement with the rest of the world in business and most other spheres of activity, American colleges have not made much headway in conveying to undergraduates enough knowledge of other languages and other cultures to give them the international background they will need for their careers. A number of institutions have experimented with overseas programs of different types. But only 60,000 out of 12 million American students study abroad each year, many fewer, proportionately, than in other advanced countries and far below the almost 400,000 foreign students enrolled in our colleges and universities. American students also lag behind their counterparts in other industrialized nations in their knowledge of foreign cultures and their ability to speak foreign languages. "It seems that repeated efforts to address this [educational challenge]," states a recent Social Science Research Council study, "have been of limited effectiveness because of the enormity of the problem, the immense dispersion of the educational system, and the lack of agreement on just what the content of that knowledge and understanding should be and to whom it should be given, when, where, and how."[1] The same study has equally harsh words for the teaching of foreign languages. Although instructional technique has improved, "the skills it imparts are too low and too scholastic; the languages taught were appropriate for the nineteenth century but not for the twenty-first; the ways of measuring skill acquisition are outmoded."[2] Oddly enough, fewer colleges require language instructions today than was true twenty-five years ago even though the need has hardly diminished.

In advanced education and research, our regional and international centers are probably no stronger, and may be even less so, than they were twenty years ago. Very few of these centers have joint programs with business schools or with other professional faculties. More troubling still, the quality of international scholars seems to have declined in the last decade or two, with serious shortages of outstanding specialists in such important fields as the Soviet economy, development economics, and international law.

The record is no more encouraging in the case of business schools. During the past quarter century, the best faculties have been much more influenced by the standards of the academy than by the practical needs of business. According to a recent report on management education: "Perhaps our most disturbing finding was the general absence of concern for, or even expressions of awareness of, looming changes in the environment in which business schools will be operating in the next 10–15 years."[3] Most leading schools have chosen to emphasize the academic disciplines of economics, mathematics, and statistics and their applications to areas of business, such as finance and accounting, that lend themselves to "hard" quantitative methods. Much less attention has been paid to "softer" subjects, such as doing business in foreign countries, motivating employees, using technology effectively, improving productivity and quality control in manufacturing, or creating more fruitful relationships with government.

Until very recently, at least, the fact that these topics happened to be highly relevant to the effort to keep American business competitive seems to have mattered very little to most curriculum committees. Small wonder: few of their members have graduated from business schools, let alone had any experience in a corporation. Most faculty members in the best-known schools have been recruited more for their research capabilities in established academic disciplines than for their knowledge of business. Professors of this type have tended to put less emphasis on teaching than on research and to resort to lecturing rather than using cases and problems that will help their students to integrate and apply knowledge to solve real problems. Many instructors simply teach their native disciplines, such as economics, statistics, or decision theory, leaving it to students to learn for themselves how to apply this knowledge to solve actual business problems.

Something similar has occurred in our leading engineering faculties. Professors in these schools have been influenced heavily by the tendency in modern science to emphasize basic new discoveries and, in applied fields, to favor the search for new products over attempts to improve existing products and manufacturing processes. According to a recent report from MIT, "Applied science came to dominate the nation's leading engineering schools. Excellence in engineering science became the principal criterion for faculty tenure and promotion. At the same time, the design of manufacturing processes and production operations acquired a reputation as lowbrow activities and largely disappeared from the curriculum."[4] In the words of a past president of the National Academy of Engineering, Eric A. Walker, graduates of engineering schools with the typical contemporary curriculum "resemble research scientists more than they [do] engineers able to design and manufacture turbines, generators, transformers, and internal combustion engines. . . . A wholesale return to the basics in engineering education will be necessary before the United States can begin to reclaim its position of preeminence in the world marketplace."[5] Fortunately, new programs in manufacturing have begun to emerge in the last few years, as companies have become more aware of their competitive difficulties and more anxious to recruit students interested in production. Still, the response is belated at best, so that its full benefit for American industry will not be felt for some time to come.

The record of our law schools is somewhat more mixed. With respect to competitiveness, law faculties have paid little attention in their research to the effects of regulation or to methods of reducing regulatory costs. The pervasive emphasis in legal education has been on abstract reasoning in pursuit of ideals such as justice, equality, liberty, and order rather than on practical efforts to achieve greater efficiency and speed in resolving disputes. Legal scholars have shown so little interest in empirical work on the actual behavior of the legal system and its impact on industry that there is scant prospect that law schools will play a significant role in finding ways to improve efficiency by minimizing regulatory and legal burdens.

In contrast, the record of law schools in the area of poverty has been much better. Most faculties offer a variety of courses in this field, broadly defined, and almost all have clinical programs that allow students to help provide legal services to indigent clients. If there is a deficiency, it is the paucity of empirical studies by law professors to examine the impact of law on poor people and to seek more efficient ways to meet their legal needs.

Universities have done a much less satisfactory job of helping to improve the quality of government. Despite the pressing need for able officials, schools of public administration have long been low on the totem pole on most campuses, far beneath such professional schools as law, business, medicine, and engineering. Several leading universities offer no programs at all to prepare for careers in government. Within the past twenty years, new schools of public policy have attracted some attention, but they have not yet won a prominent place in many universities. Rarely are they given resources at anything like the level supplied to the major professional faculties. Often, they are merged with business schools, which invariably dominate them in funding, faculty strength, and student enrollments.

Schools of education also rank far down on the typical campus hierarchy. In the world outside, it is striking to observe how little these faculties have counted in the national debate over school reform. Indeed, since the debate began, several universities have even moved to cut back or eliminate their schools or departments of education. In those that remain, faculty salaries are generally low, classes are overcrowded, and morale tends to be poor. Too often, such schools are content to attract large numbers of students who can be taught at low cost in order to generate the funds to finance more prestigious forms of discipline-based research.

Finally, work on poverty and its attendant ills has likewise received insufficient attention in the last twenty years. During the War Against Poverty in the 1960s, research on these subjects boomed and government funds for this purpose continued to rise through most of the 1970s. Nevertheless, poverty as a subject rarely attracted the ablest, most widely respected scholars. Moreover, even before the sharp decline of federal research funds in the 1980s, the volume of research was small in comparison to the efforts mounted in the more important fields of science and health. It is not surprising, then, that we still lack much of the knowledge we need to devise effective programs to overcome a gigantic social problem that stunts the lives of millions and gravely hampers the progress of the economy.

Schools of social work are similarly neglected. Like faculties of education, they are poor stepchildren on most university campuses. Beset by declining enrollments, internal disputes over aims and methods, and attacked even by alumni practitioners, they have not managed to give effective leadership to their profession. Indeed, their professors are often accused of being more concerned with research that will win them status in the academy than with studying firsthand the problems of poor people in urban ghettos.

The record just described is troubling. Again and again, universities have put a low priority on the very programs and initiatives that are needed most to increase productivity and competitiveness, improve the quality of government, and overcome the problems of illiteracy, miseducation, and unemployment. As a result, universities have accomplished far less than they appear to be capable of achieving. The immediate question is why. Only by answering that question will we come to understand what universities can and should do to improve upon their record.

Explaining the Universities' Performance

If one were to ask the average person why universities have not done a better job of responding to the challenge of competitiveness, poverty, and related social needs, the most common reply would undoubtedly be that universities are "ivory towers," too detached from society to be keenly concerned about its problems. This answer reflects a widespread misimpression about universities. In fact, the opposite is more nearly correct.

The influence of the outside world. Higher education has to pay close attention to the larger society because it is among the most competitive enterprises in America. More than 3,000 separate colleges and universities are perpetually vying with one another for students, faculty, and resources. This constant rivalry generates powerful forces that make universities pay attention to the desires and priorities of many groups and constituencies in the outside world. In order to recruit enough students of sufficient quality, faculties must create educational and extracurricular programs that respond to the desires and ambitions of young people and their parents. The intense competition for scientists and scholars means that universities must strive mightily to attract the ablest faculty and equip them with the best obtainable facilities to perform the kinds of research that society will pay for. The struggle to obtain funding for research, for buildings, and for new and better programs forces higher education to adapt to priorities established by foundations, government agencies, corporations, and other donors. If anything, therefore, higher education in the United States is influenced too much by the outside world rather than too little. Indeed, some would argue that it is precisely this influence that accounts for the failure of universities to respond better to urgent national needs.

According to this argument, it is no accident that universities have failed to address the issues of poverty and competitiveness more effectively, for universities are captive to the very social values and priorities that caused these problems in the first place. The vocations that attract the best students, and hence command a high priority in research universities, are rarely the careers most essential to improving competitiveness or attending to many other important social questions. Industry has traditionally given less pay and prestige to industrial engineers skilled in manufacturing and design than to those interested in research. Hence, it is not surprising that faculties of engineering have adopted the same priorities. Few corporations pay a premium to students who speak foreign languages or have worked overseas, even though American executives sent abroad have a higher failure rate than those of any of our principal competitors.[6] Under these conditions, there is little incentive to acquire international competence.

In much the same way, communities throughout the nation have tended to pay their public school teachers and government officials much less than the salaries available to talented graduates entering the private sector. While corporate executives and lawyers have seen their compensation rise by more than 50 percent in constant dollars over the past decade, teachers' salaries have only recently returned to the levels they achieved in the late 1960s. Real salaries of high federal officials have actually declined by a startling 30–40 percent or more during the same period. The result is that faculties of education and public administration attract less talented students who are less interesting to teach than young people entering schools of law, business, or medicine, and who are less likely after graduation to make the generous donations needed to build strong professional schools. Even students of business administration receive the most lucrative offers from consulting firms and investment banking concerns that need young people with strong quantitative and analytic skills. Responding to these incentives, over 50 percent of all Harvard Business School graduates took jobs in such enterprises in 1987, while only 22 percent took jobs with manufacturing companies. Is it really surprising, then, that many business school faculties have chosen to emphasize quantitative and financial skills over training in production or design?

Similar reasons, one can argue, help account for the insufficient effort devoted to the problems of poverty, regulatory costs, education, adult illiteracy, and the like. Serious investigation of these issues is expensive, and money must be raised to finance the research. Without a constant and substantial flow of funds, good scholars and students will not be attracted to the field and intellectual progress will be inhibited. Yet in contrast to research in most fields of science and medicine, the money available for research on social problems has fluctuated widely from one period to another. The same is true of funding for schools of education, social work, or human services. The last ten years have been particularly austere. Even before President Reagan took office, poverty as a field no longer received a high priority from the federal government. Since 1978, the research budget of the Department of Education has dropped by more than 70 percent. Few private foundations have set aside substantial fractions of their resources for work on these topics, and corporations and individual donors are rarely interested. Small wonder, then, that the very best students and scholars have turned to other fields where prospects of support seem brighter.

Both in teaching and in research, therefore, universities are responsive, but what they respond to is what the society chooses to pay for, not what it most needs. The two are not exactly the same. As we have seen, the careers that command the highest salaries and attract the brightest students are not necessarily the vocations that most observers consider to be the most important for the betterment of society. Or more precisely, prevailing patterns of compensation do not do a particularly good job of distributing talent in accordance with society's needs. As for research, although the multitude of funding sources in America undoubtedly helps to ensure that no important social need is overlooked entirely, our decentralized system offers no guarantee that available funds will be allocated in the proportions needed to yield the greatest gains to the society. Personal preferences, political pressures, and narrow time horizons all create irrational patterns of funding, such as the billions spent on finding a cure for cancer compared with the pittance made available to find effective ways of inducing people to stop smoking. These vagaries do much to distort the efforts of universities to respond to society's problems.

Intellectual influences. Persuasive as it seems, the view just described does not fully account for the actions of our academic institutions. For example, law schools have devoted much effort to the problems of poverty although there are no high-paying jobs in the field and few affluent donors interested in this type of work. Conversely, many businessmen would gladly support expanded efforts to discover how to enhance employee motivation or improve industrial processes and design, while many others would underwrite research by legal scholars to explore ways of reducing regulatory costs. Yet all these fields have languished.

Such anomalies are enough to embolden skeptics to ask whether other forces may be more responsible than outside funding for the slow progress in so many areas of work related to important national needs. Intellectual factors offer an alternative explanation. According to this theory, subjects that attract outstanding teachers and scholars are generally ones that are susceptible to verifiable experiments, or ones that some new paradigm or theory has enlivened with fresh opportunities for research, or ones that at least offer well-accepted standards of quality and peer evaluation. Yet most of the neglected topics relating to poverty and competitiveness require forms of inquiry that lack these characteristics. The problems involved tend to be so value-laden or so intractable that one must wonder whether they will yield important, verifiable results even to sustained intellectual effort.

For example, one can argue plausibly that business school subjects such as human relations, doing business abroad, or managing technology attract less attention from the leading scholars because they are all much softer topics than finance, accounting, or strategic modelling. In the latter fields, investigators can manipulate data by the application of sophisticated quantitative techniques. Since quantitative work permits greater precision and provides at least the illusion of demonstrable progress, it is more attractive to the brightest minds and lends itself more readily to rigorous teaching. In contrast, because the softer subjects are often bound up with political preferences or with the vagaries of human nature, it is much harder to develop convincing theories and harder still to verify them in practice.*

One can make a similar case that the effort to prepare school-teachers does not attract the most talented faculty because it must leave the more orderly world of developmental psychology, with its crafted experiments and carefully documented results, and face the messier, more practical challenge of helping real children learn in real schools. Likewise, in the field of public administration, progress was stymied until recently by the stubborn intellectual problem of devising a curriculum adequate for the huge variety of jobs that fit within the capacious tent of government service. More recently, the growth and spread of analytic techniques for addressing policy problems have helped to overcome this obstacle and give new life to these faculties. Yet schools of public policy have still not succeeded entirely, since they have not yet demonstrated what they can teach students about the many policy issues that do not lend themselves to quantitative analysis. Nor have they managed to find effective ways of instructing students in the unruly arts of public management where problems cannot readily be cast in forms susceptible to mathematical methods or logical demonstration.

Obstacles of an intellectual nature can also affect research priorities. In engineering, for example, problems involving the design and improvement of production processes are not considered as intellectually challenging as opportunities to design new products or, better yet, solve problems of basic science. On the other hand, inquiries into other pressing issues, such as adult

---

*Intellectual problems of a somewhat different kind inhibit student interest in the study of foreign languages, which has languished not because the outside world considers it unimportant, nor because of any lack of pedagogic techniques, but because students rarely know in college what languages they will need in later life.

illiteracy, school administration, or the organization of work, are often confounded by problems of human behavior and motivation. These characteristics make them much less susceptible to rigorous methods of research than fields such as basic science or mathematical modelling.

Other important topics call for multidisciplinary inquiry that faculty members are often ill-equipped to undertake. In studying the burdens of regulation, for example, very few law professors are trained to carry out the empirical work required to explore these problems. As a result, the intellectual barriers they face seem daunting enough to cause them to shift their efforts to other fields. Similar obstacles hinder progress in subjects such as chronic unemployment or poverty where economics needs to draw upon the behavioral sciences to probe the causes and possible cures. The study of competitiveness itself suffers from the difficulty of mounting a comprehensive inquiry that draws upon all of the disciplines needed to understand the problem fully.

The preceding arguments suggest that intellectual factors do play a role in accounting for the way in which effort is distributed throughout the university. But it would be wrong to regard those factors as dominant. Ample funding remains important, often more so. How else can we explain why business and law schools have attracted larger and better faculties than schools of public administration or education? It would be difficult to argue that the problems of corporate management are so much more amenable to teaching and research than those of public management. Or that constitutional law is any more rigorous and verifiable than the analysis of curricula and education policies.

What, then, can we say about the relative importance of outside support and intellectual appeal in shaping the priorities of the university? It is difficult to answer this question because outside support and intellectual appeal often complement each other in mutually reinforcing ways. For example, a shortage of funding will frequently discourage the most promising scholars from entering a field and thereby impede intellectual progress. The effect will often be to make the subject *seem* less promising than it actually is, which further discourages talented students and financial support. Ample supplies of funding can easily have the opposite result. Conversely, the intellectual difficulties that dog the investigation of many important questions frequently serve to discourage outside support, just as the intellectual excitement generated by opening up a new field will tend to attract able scholars and students and then bring greater outside funding as well. In all these cases, it is impossible to say whether money or intellectual appeal is the dominant force; they are so interdependent that one cannot disentangle the precise influence of either.

Despite these complications, there are several things that are generally true about the relative influence of money and subject matter. Obviously, the availability of outside funds becomes essential whenever the research and education required are expensive. But money is not always sufficient to guarantee an effective response. In some cases, a field may languish despite the prospect of substantial outside support because the intellectual difficulties are simply too great. For example, since legal scholars are untrained to do empirical work, it would take a great deal of money, work, and pressure to induce law faculties to reconstitute themselves to mount a strong, continuing research effort of this kind. Similarly, one should not expect large-scale research programs on the possibility of life after death, or even of life on other planets, despite the keen interest in the outside world for enlightenment on these subjects. The problems are simply too difficult.

In other instances it is possible to do serious teaching and research on a given subject, but the problems involved are not intellectually interesting. In this event, the mere possibility of outside support may not trigger a response unless it is accompanied by a pressing demand for such work. The long dormancy of international business and production engineering offers an apt example. Now that so many complaints have been voiced about the neglect of these subjects, engineering and business faculties are responding. But they did not react without special prodding, and the reason they did not was because the subjects involved lacked intellectual appeal to their faculties. Even now the response is quite guarded. Most business schools, for example, list a course or two in international business, but the changes have not been great enough to endanger the primacy or the working habits of the more traditional faculty.

The force of these inhibitions is especially clear when the cost of needed reforms is not great enough for outside funding to be a decisive factor. It does not take much money to add more international courses to the undergraduate curriculum or to add courses on poverty to a law school's curriculum. In such instances, if action is not forthcoming the reasons are likely to be intellectual rather than financial in nature.

Academic values. Until now, we have looked at the intellectual appeal of different questions solely in terms of the intrinsic features of the problems involved—for example, their difficulty and verifiability. These characteristics are doubtless important. But the appeal of a subject to teachers and scholars is a more complex, more subjective matter. It is made up not only of the demonstrable intellectual characteristics of a topic but of a congeries of other factors that are harder to weigh and cannot be accounted for solely on rational grounds. Instead, academic priorities are also shaped by a broad consensus in the academy on the kinds of intellectual work that matter most.

This consensus is not only shared by most faculty members, it is enshrined in the measures that determine the reputation of a university both in the academic and the outside worlds. Reputation is important in attracting students, faculty, and funding, and therefore is crucial to the success of academic institutions and their leaders. Its measurement, however, is notoriously inexact. Experience suggests that it has something to do with such matters as a university's success in attracting able students (measured by standardized test scores and national award winners), and in recruiting to the faculty Nobel Prize winners and members of elite organizations such as the National Academy of Science. Even more important is a university's standing in national surveys of professors on the quality of graduate and professional faculties throughout the country. It is fashionable to scoff at these surveys and to criticize their patent methodological weaknesses. Crude as they are, however, they are the only widely publicized measures that we have, and academic leaders take them seriously.

The most significant thing to note about these surveys is that they are influenced primarily by the views of professors, views that reflect deeply ingrained beliefs about what is most important in academic work. Among these beliefs is the conviction that the disciplines of arts and sciences, and the colleges and graduate programs in which these disciplines are rooted, are the most important part of the university. Another widely held opinion is that faculties of law, medicine, business, and perhaps engineering are more important than other professional schools, such as education, public administration, and social work. Finally, at least in leading universities, research is valued over teaching, and pure research gains more respect than applied research aimed at solving problems in the real world. Of course, those who believe most strongly in the overriding importance of pure research are not uncaring about society and its needs. They simply feel that universities will make their greatest contribution to society by seeking knowledge for its own sake, leaving to others the task of applying the results to help solve practical problems.

The prevailing consensus about what kinds of academic work matter most results in part from forces we have already discussed. For example, the importance of the basic sciences reflects not only their impact on the outside world but the degree to which their subject matter lends itself to progress through systematic experiment and verification. The primacy of law, business, and medicine among the professional schools is largely due to the high quality of students and faculty they attract, which in turn results from the enviable status of these professions in the society and the affluence of their alumni.

Still, academic priorities reflect something more than the intellectual promise of different fields of knowledge or the degrees of support they command in the larger society. Beyond these factors lie influences peculiar to the academy—its history and traditions, its time-honored criteria for recognition and reward, its long-standing ambivalence toward attempts to solve the practical problems of society, and above all, its commitment to other aims such as the preservation and enhancement of our culture and the continuing quest to comprehend nature and the human predicament. These beliefs help to explain, to take but one example, why most universities will struggle to maintain excellent programs in French literature but allow programs on poverty to languish (even though the former subject lends itself to scientific verification even less than the latter and attracts even less outside support). In the last analysis, French literature serves other ends that give it a higher standing in the academy's traditional scale of values than policy-oriented research on poverty.

This scale of values has a powerful impact on the way universities distribute their energies and resources, not only because it reflects deep-seated feelings within the academy but also because it affects how faculties, deans, and presidents will be judged by their peers and by the outside world. Although the values themselves were developed in the leading research universities, they affect the behavior of a far greater number of academic institutions anxious to achieve higher levels of recognition and prestige. The net result is a set of pervasive academic priorities that do not correspond well to the pressing problems of the society. A university's reputation is not much enhanced by developing better programs for preparing teachers, by strengthening curricula in industrial engineering and design, by building a school of public administration, or by creating research programs in adult illiteracy or school dropouts. These subjects may occasionally attract public notice but they are not where the greatest academic distinction lies. As a result, university officials who contemplate such efforts will have to recognize not only that it will be difficult to raise funds and to attract gifted students and faculty but also that their labors will often add little to the stature of the institution. To harried presidents and deans, badgered by constant demands to raise money and resolve daily problems, these prospects will often seem discouraging enough to keep them from making an attempt.

It is important to emphasize, of course, that academic priorities *should not* correspond exactly to national needs. Many fields of inquiry have a deserved claim on academic priorities and resources because they serve important aims that have little to do with addressing society's immediate concerns. Other subjects of genuine social importance are properly ignored because they are simply not ripe for serious research or teaching. It is the essence of wise academic administration to consider these matters carefully in establishing sound priorities for the institution.

Yet even after giving due weight to such considerations, the fact remains that most universities exhibit a pattern of effort that seems uncomfortably out of line with the nation's needs. In principle, there is no convincing intellectual justification for allowing schools of education and public administration to lag so far behind schools of law and business; no valid reason why management faculties should have paid so little attention to production, human relations, or international business; no compelling logic that either keeps law schools from doing more to probe the actual effects of regulation or that prevents social scientists from paying as much attention to issues of poverty and education as biomedical investigators give to the mysteries of cancer and AIDS. Underlying these priorities are decisions made by funding sources, faculty members, and students. These are individual choices, social choices, that neither constitute a justification for the status quo nor provide a convincing reason for its perpetuation. Rather, they reflect human judgments that allow at least the possibility of reform. Before exploring ways of improving on the present situation, however, we must ask how universities have responded to still another problem that bears in fundamental ways on the quality of American society.

CHAPTER THREE

The Demise and Rebirth of Moral Education

W e have seen that strengthening the economy requires more than an effort to quicken the pace of technological progress or to improve the quality of management; it calls for a revitalization of the entire society—its government, its schools, its disadvantaged communities. In turn, the vitality of a society rests on more than the knowledge and abilities of its public officials, business leaders, engineers, and skilled workers; it is affected at least as much by the values and attitudes of the people. We have prospered as a nation by relying on individual freedom and market-oriented competition. But we have also found that freedom must be tempered by self-restraint if we are to maintain security, guarantee opportunity for all, and build the trust required to enable people to work together effectively. We have likewise come to realize that competition, even when properly limited by laws and regulations, cannot succeed by itself in alleviating poverty, improving public education, or making us successful participants in the world economy. To achieve these goals, we need to link individualism and competition with a set of qualities of a very different kind—qualities of a more cooperative and communal nature rooted in a strong sense of personal responsibility toward institutions, communities, and other human beings.

The needed sense of responsibility begins with family, the

most immediate community to which we owe a duty. This obligation is a matter of importance not only to the family members themselves but to the entire society. Parents, if they choose to make the effort, will normally have a greater influence than anyone else on the attitudes of their children—their ethical standards, their respect for rules, their concern for others, their motivations and self-discipline. Parents also have important effects on the education of their offspring not only by creating a stimulating environment at home but also by the interest they show in their children's homework and the activities of their children's school. Indeed, a recent study comparing hundreds of effective and ineffective schools revealed that the single most important factor explaining the success of the better schools was *not* the amounts of money spent per pupil, nor the quality of the facilities, nor even the role played by the principal and teachers, but the degree of involvement by the parents.[1]

Another form of personal responsibility involves the obligations we assume at work, especially the obligations we owe to those who depend on our performance, be they clients, colleagues, superiors, or subordinates. These responsibilities—to tell the truth, to keep one's word, to make reasonable efforts to help others in need—are important to the effectiveness of all organizations, including schools and corporations. Recent research suggests that the most successful schools are those with strong, trusting partnerships between principals and teachers.[2] Similarly, unless a company's employees consider their management to be honest, reliable, and concerned for their welfare, productivity is likely to suffer. People will simply not be as loyal to the organization or feel as much responsibility to help achieve its goals as they would otherwise. The Soviet Union exhibits this phenomenon in a spectacularly disastrous form, but good and bad examples abound in every economy, including our own.

A third form of responsibility has to do with our attitudes

toward the surrounding community and, especially, toward the poor, the illiterate, the unemployed, and others in need of help. Only the government can mobilize the huge sums required to provide poor people with the essentials of food, shelter, and medical care and see to it that these benefits are available to all who deserve them. But no government program, however well designed, can respond to all the human needs of poor communities without the aid of countless individuals and voluntary organizations who offer help of a kind that public agencies cannot or will not provide: lawyers who make an effort to represent indigent clients, companies that adopt an urban school, church groups that organize a homeless shelter, professionals who find the time to counsel disadvantaged youths or work in drug rehabilitation clinics.

The last, critical form of individual responsibility is the responsibility we take as citizens to improve the quality of government. Whether by providing education, regulating business, working to reduce poverty and crime, maintaining our national security, or acting in a host of other ways that affect our critical interests, government agencies perform essential functions that the private sector cannot supply. Thus, the quality of government is a matter of the greatest importance for all of the social problems we have discussed.

It is common sport today to criticize public officials and to complain as though the actions of government were some independent force for which the public bears no responsibility. But in a democracy, the quality of government is always a reflection of the public's attitudes. It is the people who determine what type of individuals choose to enter government, what they will be paid, what their mandate will be, and what resources they can have to carry out their tasks. Thus, the willingness of individual citizens to enter public service, to compensate their officials adequately, to support programs that address significant national problems, and to pay the taxes to fund important state activities is the decisive factor determining the effectiveness of government.

Although it is always hard to generalize, there is disturbing evidence to suggest that most forms of responsibility toward others have eroded in recent decades. The record with respect to family obligations seems especially clear. Since 1960, the divorce rate has tripled with the result that over 50 percent of all marriages now end in divorce, desertion, or separation.[3] More than one-half of all divorced husbands pay no support whatsoever to their wives and children, while only one-third pay support in full even when ordered to do so by a court (and this percentage has been falling).[4] The time that parents spend with their offspring has likewise been dropping for several generations, while the hours children devote to watching television have increased to consume more time than any activity besides sleeping. Accompanying this growing parental neglect are alarming increases of up to 100 and even 200 percent in the incidence among teenagers of drug and alcohol abuse, pregnancy, suicide, and crime over the past twenty to thirty years.[5] A large majority of American adults now admit that they are not as willing as their parents were to make sacrifices for their children. These findings suggest that the family is no longer commonly regarded as the unit to which we owe our primary loyalty. Instead, more and more people seem to view it merely as a convenient arrangement to be discarded when it grows too burdensome.

Parents also seem to be taking less interest in their children's schools. Now that almost half of all children spend some of their young years in single-parent homes and more and more families have two working parents, teachers feel that they get less help than before from fathers and mothers in seeing to it that children do their homework or even attend school regularly. Indeed, between one-quarter and one-third of all boys and girls beginning school are latchkey children with no one to greet them when they come home in the afternoon.[6] Apart from parents, it is more difficult than ever to persuade good candidates to run for local school boards and even harder to induce the public to take an interest. In New York City, for example, only 6 *percent* of all eligible voters bothered to cast a ballot in the 1989 school board elections, a figure not significantly out of line with results in many other cities.

It is harder to pinpoint just what has been happening to ethical behavior in the workplace. White-collar crime has certainly risen dramatically in recent decades, but no one can be sure how much of the increase has been due to changes in legal rules or in the priorities of law enforcement officials. We seem to read more and more newspaper stories of business takeovers, gargantuan executive salaries, exorbitant fees for lawyers and other middlemen, and other signs of rampant greed, but these scattered accounts scarcely amount to hard evidence.

What *does* seem clear is that large majorities of the public *believe* that ethical standards in the workplace, especially among corporate leaders, have declined. The percentage of people who feel that most individuals in power try to take advantage of others has doubled over the last two decades and now exceeds 60 percent. Large majorities believe that corporations do not see to it that their executives behave ethically. Fewer than one-third of employees now believe that management is trustworthy.[7]

Such cynicism and distrust may seem surprising in light of the widely publicized efforts of many companies to develop more participatory styles of management evincing greater concern for the opinions and welfare of employees. Such practices do indeed appear to be spreading, spurred by the demands of a more educated, independent work force and by the examples of successful Japanese companies. But in the end these methods will succeed only to the extent that management genuinely cares about its employees, takes its obligations toward them seriously, and does not merely try to manipulate workers to achieve greater productivity. To date, opinion surveys seem to suggest that many employees are not yet convinced that their employers are sincere. Thus, a recent *Time* survey suggests that almost two-thirds of the respondents believe that workers are less loyal to their employers today than they were ten years ago; similarly, over twice as many workers believe that companies have become less loyal to their employees as believe the opposite.[8]

There is greater cause for optimism regarding grass-roots volunteer activity. Surveys show that Americans have gradually been getting more involved in community service through churches, corporations, and civic groups of all kinds. The number of participants has now reached 45 million, a postwar high. Still, barely 40 percent of all adults participate even today, and the average amount of time spent by volunteers is only two hours per week.[9] Despite all the volunteers, the services rendered fall manifestly short of meeting the need. For example, bar associations are considering rules to make it mandatory for all lawyers to serve a minimum number of hours every year to help the poor, since the needs for legal services far exceed the supply. "With the [huge] salaries we have to pay our young associates," claimed a partner in one large firm, "we can't afford to let them spend time doing *pro bono* work."

Attitudes toward government are much more worrisome. Repeated scandals and misadventures over twenty years have alienated many people and sapped their confidence in the probity and effectiveness of public officials. People still want a government that performs a broad range of important responsibilities; more than 75 percent resist any cuts in social programs.[10] Yet over 80 percent of the public oppose any rise in taxes—and this despite the well-known fact that current revenues are not sufficient to pay for existing programs.[11]

Although the public wants the government to carry out a vast array of vital, complicated tasks, it also refuses to support adequate compensation for key public servants. Over the past twenty years, real salaries of top federal officials have declined by more than 40 percent and there is fierce grass-roots sentiment against efforts to make up the lost ground. It is convenient to explain these tendencies by calling attention to our budgetary deficits and the consequent need to cut government expenditures. Yet the percentage of America's national income that is taken in taxes of all kinds is virtually the *lowest* among all industrial nations.[12] The fact is that the public is simply unwilling to pay for what it wants and needs from government. In addition, people seem less and less willing to participate even in the most important political elections. Despite massive efforts by both parties to register new voters, participation in the last presidential campaign dwindled to 50 percent, the lowest proportion of any advanced, democratic nation in the world.

In sum, there is much evidence to suggest an erosion of many forms of personal responsibility that are essential to overcoming our most pressing national problems. Such feelings of personal obligation typically arise from a broad, ethical sense of concern for others which develops best in an atmosphere of trust that others are behaving ethically and responsibly in return. At a time when these attitudes of trust and moral concern seem weakened and precarious, it is important to ask how they can be strengthened and what higher education can contribute to the process.

From this standpoint universities occupy strategic ground. Almost half of the population, including nearly all of our public officials, business executives, civic leaders, and professionals, enter our colleges and professional schools. For several formative years the university is the dominant influence in their lives.

The young people who flock to our colleges and universities are not immune to the worrisome trends in moral and social responsibility throughout America. The proportion of college students who admit to having cheated in class seems to have risen appreciably over the past three decades.[13] Other surveys have found that undergraduates are growing less altruistic and more preoccupied with self-serving goals. In polls of entering freshmen over the past fifteen to twenty years, the values that have risen most are the desire to be "very well-off financially," to gain personal recognition, and to "have administrative responsibility for the work of others." In contrast, students show no growth or an actual decline in their interest in such other values as the desire to keep up-to-date in political affairs, to participate in community action programs, or to help clean up the environment.[14] There is also evidence that less than 5 percent of the ablest college students are prepared to consider government service as their preferred career and that the percentage of eighteen- to twenty-four-year-olds who actually vote is consistently lower and has fallen faster than that of any other age group.[15]

These trends underscore the need for universities to provide a sound moral education in the broadest sense of the term—that is, to help students adopt higher ethical standards and a stronger sense of communal and civic responsibility. But what should universities do—indeed, what can they do—to respond effectively to this challenge? As we will discover, such questions have produced very different answers over the history of American higher education. In recent years they have provoked a particularly odd debate in which neither side seems to hear what the other is saying.

The Older Tradition

Until this century, educators in Europe and America not only sought to build the character of their students; they made this task their central preoccupation. As Plato observed, "If you ask what is the good of education, the answer is easy—that education makes good men, and that good men act nobly."[16] In the New World, Harvard and our other oldest colleges were founded to prepare ministers and civic leaders of firm conviction and upright character. By the eighteenth century, instructors had added moral philosophy to Bible study—to the consternation of Cotton Mather—but the principal aim was still to develop "good men" or, in Jefferson's words, "an aristocracy of talent and virtue." As Jefferson conceived it, such education would not merely promote morality and a decent respect for the rights of others; it would also "form the statesmen, legislators, and judges on whom the public prosperity and individual happiness are so much to depend."[17]

These tendencies continued strongly into the nineteenth century. President Francis Wayland of Brown echoed the feelings of many leading educators of his time when he observed: "The most important end to be secured in the education of the young is moral character."[18] In building character, Wayland and presidents like him placed great store by the study of philosophy. Its teachings had several purposes: to integrate all knowledge into a coherent, intelligible whole; to reconcile religion and science (or at least to prevent science from undermining religion); and to discover moral precepts that could be forcefully conveyed to students for application in their personal and professional lives. The effort to impart these moral laws and impress them on the behavior of students pervaded the entire life of the college. During chapel services, presidential addresses, and other ceremonial occasions, students were constantly urged to live god-fearing, upright lives.

These exhortations were backed by detailed codes of conduct enforced by fines, demerits, and, if need be, expulsion. Faculty members played a prominent role in policing conduct and administering discipline. As one Yale alumnus, William Phelps, described it: "When I was an undergraduate, it was part of every instructor's duty, if he had a room on the campus, to maintain order. It was not an uncommon sight, in the midst of an uproar at night, to spot a professor in his nightgown hiding behind a tree, and taking down names of those unfortunate students who were revealed by the bonfire."[19]

The effort to mold conduct through discipline was not notably successful. Annual reports of Harvard presidents in the 1840s are spiced with references to episodes such as "college fence and small building were wantonly set on fire and burned down"[20] or "a bomb shell was placed, about midnight, in one of the rooms in University Hall and exploded, doing great damage."[21] More than a few Harvard students, according to historian Bernard Bailyn, "were seen loafing around Boston smoking, drinking and whoring."[22] To cope with these transgressions, the book of regulations at the end of the Civil War took a full forty pages of text. President Everett personally administered discipline by reproving students for misdeeds as trifling as "casting reflections with a looking glass on the face of a lady passing through the Yard." With the help of the College tutors, he graded all undergraduates on a "scale of merit" that combined marks for personal behavior with grades for academic achievement. Eventually, these burdens proved so onerous that Everett, like his successor Jared Sparks, felt compelled to resign prematurely.

Elaborate codes of conduct were the natural outgrowth of a larger effort to stress the importance of self-control and self-discipline in developing character. In the words of President Noah Porter of Yale: "To hold the student to minute fidelity in little things is an enforcement of one of the most significant maxims of the Gospel."[23] William James expressed the same thought in more secular terms: "Keep the faculty of effort alive in you by a little gratuitous exercise every day. That is, be systematically ascetic or heroic in little unnecessary points, do every day or two something for no reason than that you would rather not do it, so that when the hour of dire need draws nigh, it may find you not unnerved and untrained to stand the test."[24]

In trying to shape students' character, the nineteenth-century college did not overlook the power of example. As Porter declared in his inaugural address: "The most efficient of all moral influences in a college are those which proceed from the personal characters of the instructors."[25] To this end, James McCosh of Princeton, like many presidents of his era, interviewed all candidates for faculty positions to test the soundness of their religious views. Later on, another Princeton president, Woodrow Wilson, is said to have remarked that given a choice between hiring a scholar and a gentleman, he would unhesitatingly employ the latter. Even President Eliot of Harvard, who did so much to emphasize scholarship and freedom of inquiry, put great weight on the personal qualities of prospective faculty members. As a longtime associate once recalled: "No one could for a moment accuse Mr. Eliot of indifference to scholarship or to the teaching gift, but the dominant question in his mind was always that of character."[26]

The capstone of the undergraduate experience was a course on moral philosophy commonly taught by no less a figure than the president of the college himself. According to one historian of education, D. H. Meyer, this course was "designed to tie together all the scrambled admonitions and reprimands that had theretofore been lavished on youth, to arrange them in a systematic body and offer them as the legacy of the ages to be studied, cherished, and presumably obeyed throughout life."[27] To aid in this endeavor, philosophers and educators published textbooks on "moral science" that were written to be simple, clear, and purely didactic. Ranging from issues of private morality to questions of public philosophy and civic virtue, these texts were meant to be mastered by students outside of class as a supplement to regular course lectures. Some flavor of the experience emerges from a student's recollection of what it was like to learn at the feet of President Wayland:

> The members of the class in succession [first] recited the lecture of the preceding day. . . . This exercise concluded, there was a rustling all around the room; papers were adjusted and preparation was made for writing. The President's manuscript was opened and the well-known *ahem* was the signal for all to be ready and for the work of the hour to begin. He read slowly and the class copied. All were intent to catch the thought, at any rate, and the exact phraseology, if possible. The lecture was written in full by the students in their rooms. . . . These lectures seemed to us more wonderful than anything we had ever heard. They carried all the conviction of a [scientific] demonstration.[28]

In sum, the entire undergraduate experience reflected the overriding commitment of the nineteenth-century college to strengthen the character of its students and thereby produce an educated class committed to a principled life in the service of society. While formal instruction in moral philosophy played an important role in this effort, it was only part of a much larger undertaking that affected faculty hiring, student discipline, and every other aspect of college life.

The Decline of Moral Instruction

Despite the labor invested in this moral enterprise, the edifice began to crumble as the nineteenth century wore on. Intellectually, the effort to reconcile science and religion was undermined by the publication of Darwin's *On the Origin of Species* in 1859. Not that Darwin was openly hostile to religion. He even refused Karl Marx's request to write a preface to *Das Kapital* because the book seemed godless. Yet wittingly or not, Darwin dealt a grave blow to the very foundations of religion by propounding a convincing theory of unguided change in a world that had theretofore been thought to be ruled by divine purpose.

Within the academy, the emergence of the modern research university ushered in a new intellectual environment. The creation of state universities brought a more secular attitude to higher education, while the growth of science produced increased specialization marked by fidelity to more objective methods of inquiry. As the style of intellectual discourse grew more probing and rigorous, not only in the sciences but in other disciplines as well, confidence in the earlier moral consensus began to wane. The homilies of old-style college presidents seemed more and more simplistic and out of joint with the academic spirit of the age.

The traditional approach to moral development was also vulnerable to vast changes occurring in the United States. Elaborate disciplinary rules and didactic expositions of moral precepts worked best in an academic world where students shared a common social background and came from the simpler environments of a rural, small-town America. As villages and towns grew into cities, moral restraints were harder to transmit and enforce. Immigration brought new ethnic groups with different values and backgrounds. Industrialization created ethical problems and social conflicts that the teachings of a Wayland or a Porter could not resolve.

In the face of these pressures the old ways of developing character fell into disfavor. The great courses on moral philosophy gradually disappeared as the antebellum philosopher-presidents gave way to the entrepreneurial leaders who built modern research universities. As time went on, the study of ethics fell under the sway of academic standards that gradually became more theoretical and abstract, concerned with clarifying the meaning of ethical terms, analyzing the logic and structure of moral reasoning, and comparing ethical systems rather than discussing real-life moral dilemmas. The latter seemed impenetrable and inconclusive so long as they lacked a firmer intellectual foundation. As Kai Nielsen later observed: "It [was] felt by many philosophers that the logical status of moral utterances and the nature of moral reasoning are so unclear that we cannot profitably do normative ethics until we have a far more adequate meta-ethics than we do at present."[29]

Civic education also received little attention in the twentieth-century college. Often resisted even in the nineteenth century as "too practical," it stood little chance against the rising tide of discipline-based majors and vocationally oriented undergraduate programs. Occasionally, a reformer would press for a revitalization of civic learning in the curriculum—a Woodrow Wilson at Princeton or an Alexander Meikeljohn at Wisconsin. But these initiatives were short-lived and made little impact on other American colleges.

By the Second World War, institutions of learning had not only ceased to be actively engaged in moral and civic education; they had lost their former status as an important source of moral guidance for the society. During the first half of the nineteenth century, college presidents and professors such as Mark Hopkins, James Walker, and James McCosh instructed the reading public in ethical systems and precepts that illumined private dilemmas and important social issues. One hundred years later, this mantle had passed from the academy to theologians, such as Reinhold Niebuhr, or writers and columnists, such as Walter Lippmann.

In time, the practice of looking at the personal character of candidates for faculty appointment fell into disfavor. In the wake of repeated efforts by trustees to remove professors advocating socialism or other controversial policies, faculties worried lest "character" become a cloak for screening out colleagues with unconventional views. Moreover, once scientific and scholarly distinction came to define the reputation of the university, fewer institutions were prepared to pass over a promising young scholar because of some alleged defect in attitude or personal behavior. According to a committee of Harvard professors in 1939: "A faculty made up wholly of amiable or attractive men, or even of saints, would not as such serve the purposes of a college or university."[30] Intellect and technical proficiency had decisively triumphed as the preeminent goals of the professoriate.

Even the emphasis on discipline gradually ebbed away. As early as 1869, Harvard abandoned the practice of grading students on their conduct as well as their course work. Henceforth, the faculty would take responsibility only for evaluating academic performance, leaving student behavior to deans and administrators. For the first time, the training of mind and character was separated and placed in different hands.

As the age of entering freshmen rose after the Civil War, detailed codes of conduct grew less important. At Harvard, President Eliot denounced the idea of *in loco parentis* as "an ancient fiction which ought no longer to deceive anybody."[31] In his view, "young men . . . should best be trained to self-control in freedom by letting them taste freedom and respectability within the well-guarded enclosure of college life, while mistakes may be remedied and faults may be cured, where forgiveness is always easy, and repentance never comes too late."[32] Under Eliot's administration, the book of rules shrank from forty pages to five. In 1886, compulsory chapel was abolished. With the passage of time, dress codes, Sabbath restrictions, and requirements for attending class all disappeared to the delight of undergraduates. Other colleges gradually followed suit, albeit at a slower pace.

By World War II the moral vision of the nineteenth-century college had largely evaporated in the research university and in many other academic institutions as well. True, the undergraduate experience continued to have important effects on values, but its influence lay chiefly in persuading students to become less dogmatic, more inclined to question the precepts of parents and church, more accepting of different perspectives and points of view. This emphasis suited a society which increasingly emphasized tolerance rather than adherence to any particular body of moral precepts. In a world in which so many norms were being challenged and student bodies were growing ever more diverse, educators found it hard to help inquiring undergraduates to replace their discarded dogmas with a new set of moral values. Instead, professors concentrated more and more on conveying knowledge and imparting skills, leaving students free to fashion their own beliefs and commitments amid the multiple distractions of campus life.

These developments were masked by the fact that university leaders never explicitly renounced moral development as an important aim of higher education. Such a disclaimer would have seemed irresponsible and morally callous. Rather, educators suggested that exposure to the liberal arts and proximity to faculty members committed to the highest standards of truth and intellectual integrity would be sufficient to instill a knowledge of virtue and a respect for moral principles. According to Harvard's widely discussed report, *General Education in a Free Society,* "the best way to infect the student with the zest for intellectual integrity is to put him near a teacher who is himself selflessly devoted to the truth."[33] The authors of the report went on to observe that "the college will have to confine itself to providing a proper discrimination of values (through study of the humanities, social sciences and sciences) and will trust to the Socratic dictum that the knowledge of the good will lead to a commitment to the good."[34]

There is scant evidence that these expectations were ever

fulfilled. Numerous efforts to measure the effects of college failed to reveal any deep and lasting imprint on the moral development of undergraduates. As Howard Bowen declared after reviewing scores of such studies from the 1930s, 1940s, and 1950s: "It is worth noting that the things for which the impact of college appears to be 'negative change,' 'no change,' [or] 'not ascertainable,' are precisely the dimensions usually associated with excellence of personal character."[35]

Much the same is also true of efforts to educate students as citizens. To a large degree, postwar curricular reforms, such as those expounded in Harvard's *General Education for a Free Society*, can be viewed as efforts to strengthen undergraduate education as a bulwark against totalitarian attacks. But this lofty purpose was quickly obscured by debates over how much of the curriculum could be prescribed and how to compress large quantities of information into "essential" survey courses. The rush throughout the 1960s to dismantle requirements of every kind further undermined any pretense of civic education. By the end of the decade the Carnegie Commission on Higher Education declared that "general education for citizenship" was clearly the least successful of the several principal purposes of American higher education.

The Renaissance

Toward the close of the 1960s, however, something unexpected happened. Amid the turmoil of those protest-ridden years and the further erosion of disciplinary rules, new problems emerged to rivet the public mind on moral questions. Women demanded equality and started to demonstrate for the right to have an abortion. Struggles over civil rights erupted in the South producing a flurry of legislation that included controversial programs of affirmative action. Environmentalists began to press for restrictions to limit pollution and protect natural resources.

These were highly charged issues that affected the interests of many people and evoked passionate feelings. They were also legal and legislative questions that demanded careful reasoning and public debate. As interest mounted around the country, moral philosophers, theologians, law professors, and sociologists began to express their opinions in newspaper columns and scholarly journals. A new academic concern for practical ethics had emerged.

Gradually, courses appeared in college and professional school catalogues on ethical questions affecting personal and professional behavior. Interestingly, medicine led the way even though its academic disciplines and scientific ethos seemed further than those of any of the professional schools from moral philosophy. Ethical problems simply became too pressing for physicians to ignore. The tumult over abortion was quickly joined by a host of other controversies: when to allow terminal patients to die, whether to permit test-tube babies, what standards to apply in performing medical experiments on human beings. Suddenly, hospitals saw their practices criticized in newspaper articles while doctors had to defend themselves in lawsuits. Confronted with these perils, medical deans reached out to philosophers, priests, lawyers, and whomever else they could find to lecture their students on medical ethics.

With minor variations, this pattern repeated itself in other professional schools as well. As controversies arose over political scandals, business fraud, engineering catastrophes, and fabricated newspaper stories, courses on ethics made their way into schools of business, public administration, engineering, and journalism. In law schools, following the furor over Watergate, the American Bar Association persuaded the deans to agree to make instruction on professional responsibility a requirement for admission to the bar. In colleges, too, offerings in practical ethics and moral reasoning began to creep into the undergraduate curriculum. By the late 1970s the number of such courses nationwide had risen above 10,000.

These classes, by and large, have proved to be very different from the fabled courses in moral philosophy that college presidents taught in the nineteenth century. In that era, students had little opportunity for discussion or debate. The instructor's aim was not to ask questions or to provoke thought but to foster a belief in commonly accepted moral values. Although professors did apply their ethical precepts to practical questions of the day, this was only part of "a grander effort to help form the moral character and disposition of the individual student [by] establishing a firm ground for the unifying moral principles considered so necessary for the health of the nation."[36]

In contrast, today's course on applied ethics does not seek to convey a set of moral truths but tries to encourage students to think carefully about complex moral issues. Although students may read background material on ethical theory, they also discuss practical questions that arise in personal or professional life: whether a doctor should tell parents that their teen-age daughter is having an abortion, whether corporate executives should offer bribes to foreign governments if their leading competitors do so, whether attorneys should continue to represent clients who they know are testifying falsely. The principal aim of the course is not to impart "right answers" but to make students more perceptive in detecting ethical problems when they arise, better acquainted with the best moral thought that has accumulated through the ages, and more equipped to reason about the ethical issues they will face in their own personal and professional lives.

Reactions to the "New" Ethics

While courses on ethics have made their way into the curriculum, enthusiasm has burned more brightly among alumni than within the faculty. Most professors tend to regard these offerings with tepid interest or outright skepticism. Faculty members have various reasons for being dubious. Some professors feel that applied ethics is not a true discipline and that courses in the field are lacking in rigor. Others fear that ethics instruction will fall into the hands of ideologues who will indoctrinate students with their own social beliefs. Still others believe that such courses come too late to benefit students old enough to go to college or professional school. As one business school administrator reportedly declared: "On the subject of ethics, we feel that by the time you come to us either you have them or you don't."

These arguments are gradually disappearing, for none of them has much merit. Although professional ethics is certainly not scientific, and many ethical problems do not have clearly demonstrable answers, this is equally true of many valuable staples of the curriculum, such as classes in literature, fine arts, or human relations, not to mention courses in law or business administration. Moreover, there is little evidence that teachers of applied ethics have used their courses to force their views on students and no more risk of indoctrinating undergraduates than there is in teaching political theory, sociology, or even economics. Statements to the effect that students are too old to learn ethics are equally naive. The basic disposition to obey ethical norms may emerge in early life. Even so, students have much to learn about how to apply these general norms to the puzzling moral quandaries that arise in their personal and professional lives. A young college graduate may arrive at medical school upright in character and imbued with humane concern yet still not know how to think about such dilemmas as how much truth to tell a cancer victim or how long to use technology to keep a terminally ill patient alive.*

The doubts expressed within the academy pale beside the objections of prominent conservatives. Unlike the typical faculty skeptic, most conservatives firmly believe that universities should try to strengthen the moral principles of their students. Nevertheless, they condemn the new ethics courses on several grounds. They claim that those who teach such classes are so anxious to be tolerant of differing ethical systems and creeds that students come to believe that all moral views are entitled to equal respect. They deplore the efforts of instructors not to engage in indoctrination, even to the point of refusing to endorse such basic virtues as honesty and keeping one's word. Finally, they attack teachers of applied ethics for emphasizing difficult moral dilemmas that seem to have no convincing solution, thus leaving the impression that all questions of morality are unanswerable. Because of these shortcomings, conservative critics claim that courses in practical ethics, at best, will confuse students, reinforce their ethical relativism, and fail to improve their standards

* A more troublesome problem is the dearth of well-trained instructors to offer classes in practical ethics, especially in professional schools. Such courses are difficult to teach, since they call for preparation in two entirely different subjects: ethics and some area of practical application, such as law, business, or medicine. Since no established program in a university combines instruction in both fields, most professors of practical ethics have to teach themselves an important part of what they need to know. Such preparation can often be inadequate, causing courses in practical ethics to be superficial and thereby vindicate the worst fears of their detractors. Yet even this problem is not insurmountable. Universities can create programs to train philosophers in some important areas of application, or vice versa, just as they have done in developing interdisciplinary fields such as history of science, political economy, or medical economics. Initiatives of this kind are beginning to get started on a few campuses. Now that the interest in applied ethics has grown so great, it is probably only a matter of time before more universities find ways of preparing instructors to teach such courses competently.

of behavior. At worst, it is said, participants will emerge from such classes more cynical about ethics and more clever at thinking up plausible arguments for any course of conduct they wish to follow.

William Bennett, then U.S. Secretary of Education, voiced these concerns in his typically colorful fashion when he spoke at Harvard University in October 1986. "Where are our colleges and universities," he asked, "on the issue of their responsibility to foster moral discernment in their students? With the exception of a relatively few places—mostly religious or military institutions—higher education is silent."[37] When asked about the rapid growth of courses on moral reasoning and professional ethics, he replied: "That's about [moral] dilemmas, lifeboat stuff. I don't mean theory. I meant getting drugs off campus."[38] Alas, the debate was never squarely joined, nor has it been in other forums. Bennett and his supporters seem bent on caricaturing the new courses without understanding what the instructors are actually doing. Proponents of applied ethics, on the other hand, have failed to answer Bennett's charge to look beyond the classroom and consider aspects of moral education apart from courses on ethical issues.[39]

In many ways this controversy echoes an ancient dispute dating back at least to ancient Greece.[40] In fifth century Athens, two schools of thought emerged on how to carry out the critical task of teaching ethics and civic responsibility. The traditional view relied on exhorting the young to do the proper thing and punishing them when they failed. The newer way, urged by Socrates, sought to teach people to know the good by provoking them to think about fundamental moral aims and dilemmas. Socrates argued that those who had not learned to reason about such questions could not apply their principles to the shifting circumstances they would face in later life. In this, he was surely correct. Yet Socrates sometimes talked as if knowledge alone would suffice to ensure virtuous action. He did not stress the value of early habituation, positive example, and obedience to rules in giving students the desire and self-discipline to live up to their beliefs and to respect the basic norms of behavior essential to civilized communities. For this neglect, he was savagely attacked. It fell to Aristotle to see the wisdom of combining both traditions so that young people might acquire not merely an ability to think clearly about ethical problems but the desire and will to put their conclusions into practice.

In the contemporary university, as in ancient Greece, the critical question is how to combine education in moral reasoning with a broader effort to teach by habit, example, and exhortation. The ability to reason is essential to help us make our way through all the confusing dilemmas and conflicting arguments that abound in an era when society's consensus on issues of value has disintegrated under the weight of cultural diversity, technological change, and other complexities of modern life. But moral reasoning alone may not be enough to bring us to *behave* morally. How, then, can a university go further and help students to develop the desire and the will to adhere to moral precepts in their personal and professional lives?

At this point, universities confront a serious dilemma. They can try to impart a preferred moral code by every reasonable means at their disposal: classroom instruction, exhortation by academic leaders, rules of conduct backed by discipline, and the like. If they do, they risk imposing their views on students in a manner that conflicts with principles of intellectual freedom basic to the modern university. To avoid this danger, they may elect simply to teach students to think more carefully about moral dilemmas without attempting to dictate answers. This is the method followed in most contemporary courses in applied ethics. Useful as it is, however, it runs the risk of making students clever casuists, adept at arguing any side of a difficult moral or social problem but lacking strong convictions of their own that they try to put into practice.

In short, efforts to create a serious program of moral education seem to be caught between the evils of indoctrination, on the one hand, and the hazards of ethical relativism, on the other. Escaping this dilemma is the key to success in helping students to develop stronger ethical standards and a greater concern for the welfare of others. How this can be managed and whether it can be done at all are questions that still await an answer.

CHAPTER FOUR

Toward a Contemporary Program of Moral Education

With all its snares and pitfalls, moral education has proved to be a daunting enterprise. The history of higher education is studded with efforts to develop character that, in retrospect, seem quaint, misdirected, or downright objectionable. More often than not, such ventures have either proved ineffectual or degenerated into crude attempts to impose particular doctrines or petty rules of behavior.

Despite these problems, moral education is too important to discard just because prior efforts have failed. Besides, universities cannot avoid the task whether or not they relish the responsibility. Like it or not, they will affect the moral development of their students by the ways in which they administer their rules of conduct, by the standard they set in dealing with ethical issues confronting the institution, by the manner in which they counsel their students and coach their athletic teams, indeed, even by their indifference toward moral issues in and out of the classroom. The only question is whether they choose to proceed blindly and ad hoc or with careful forethought. Let us consider, then, how an institution could construct a program to help its students to enhance not only their capacity to perceive moral issues and to think about them clearly but their resolve to act on their beliefs as well. Having described what such a program might look like, we can then ask whether the attempt is worth making.

Early Steps

A serious program of moral education must begin with the first weeks that students spend at a university, for this period is often critical in shaping their attitudes toward the institution and their expectations of what they will take away from their experience. Never again are they likely to be so attentive to what the institution says or so open to advice about what aspirations and values matter most. Yet the moment is often overlooked. Amid the mass of information handed out to entering students about courses, curricular requirements, extracurricular organizations and the like, many colleges fail to include any thoughtful exposition of the larger purposes to which this wealth of activity is directed. As a result, the institution loses an important opportunity, perhaps *the* most important opportunity, to emphasize the commitment of the college to helping its students to acquire well-considered ethical standards and strong commitments to helping others.

The same point applies to professional schools as well. Too often, students arrive at schools of business, government, medicine, or law filled with curiosity about their profession and their role within it only to be plunged immediately into the details of acquiring basic skills and knowledge. Little effort is made to consider the larger ends to which the profession is directed or the need to reconcile obligations to company, patient, or client with a greater duty to society. Indeed, such concerns are sometimes dismissed deliberately as distractions that interfere with rigorous professional analysis. As noted law professor Karl Llewellyn once declared to students:

> The hardest job of the first year is to lop off your common sense, to knock your ethics into temporary anaesthesia. Your view of social policy, your sense of justice—to knock

those out of your system along with woozy thinking, along with ideas all fuzzed along their edges. You are to acquire the ability to think precisely, to analyze coldly, to work within a body of materials that is given.[1]

Few professors today would dare say such things so explicitly. Yet much the same result occurs through studied omission and emphasis on the "practical" considerations that must guide decisions on the "real" world. Such practices often produce an atmosphere similar to the one described in the following account of a leading business school by a student who happened to be an Episcopal priest.

Privately and personally the students were warm human beings, but publicly many adopted aggressive, cynical and callous styles. In the fall we saw a movie on the coal miners' strike in Harlan County, Ky., and the sight of the over-weight miners' wives brought wave after wave of cackling derision. When, in a discussion of textile workers in England, it was revealed that a woman who had sewed for 12 years for $100 a week might lose her job, the class was almost unanimous in its feeling that she deserved to be laid off, since she was being paid too much.[2]

The environment that produces such responses is unfortunate, unnecessary, and potentially destructive. No one should begin professional school without being made to understand that to acquire special expertise is to acquire power and that it is dangerous to wield such power without learning to use it responsibly. No professional school should risk creating an impression that matters of moral and social responsibility are digressions or sentimental irrelevancies rather than integral parts of all sound analysis.

Ethics and the Curriculum

Although the traditional liberal arts curriculum may not automatically provide an adequate moral education, it undoubtedly helps in many ways to develop ethical awareness and moral reasoning. The study of literature can awaken one's conscience by making more vivid the predicament of others. Traditional courses in ethics can provide a philosophical foundation for thinking precisely about moral issues. Studying the social sciences can help students to understand a host of subjects of civic significance, such as the institutions and processes of government, the problems of the poor and disadvantaged, and the meaning of essential values such as justice, freedom, equality, legitimate authority, fair process, and their application to various public issues. Learning of this kind helps to explain why investigators find that young people continue to develop their powers of moral reasoning so long as they remain in school or university and usually cease to do so when their formal education comes to an end.[3]

Yet by themselves, traditional courses in the liberal arts do not go far enough. Neither the classics nor history have yielded a sufficiently compelling normative vision to justify the hopes of a Jowett or a Burckhardt that studying these subjects would enable students to learn how to lead a virtuous life. Humanistic disciplines have become preoccupied with other concerns, and most professors in these fields feel unqualified to teach such material. Besides, courses in the liberal arts are deliberately nonvocational and hence are unlikely to take up ethical dilemmas that arise within the professions.

These are the gaps that the new courses in applied ethics and professional responsibility seek to fill. Properly taught, they can yield important benefits. By studying problems that commonly arise in personal and professional life, students will be more likely to perceive moral dilemmas they would otherwise ignore. By finding that these dilemmas raise issues that are susceptible to careful reasoning and argument, students will be less inclined, not more, to believe that every point of view is entitled to tolerance and respect. By learning to analyze moral issues more rigorously, students will realize that many of these problems *do* have reasonably clear solutions, given basic premises that almost all human beings share. Although no classroom experience can suffice to turn a scoundrel into a virtuous human being, most young people arrive at the university with decent instincts and a genuine concern for others. For them, courses that foster an ability to detect ethical issues more perceptively, to think about them more carefully, to understand more clearly the reasons for acting morally seem likely not only to train their minds but to have some positive effect on their behavior as well. Such empirical evidence as there is tends to confirm this supposition.*

*There is little correlation between ethical *beliefs* and ethical *behavior*. Countless experiments have confirmed what common sense would tell us: that a host of circumstances—personal danger, fear of disapproval, lack of forethought, the urging of others, the presence of fatigue or stress—can keep people from putting their convictions into practice. Yet a number of studies have found not only that discussion courses in applied ethics have a modest but positive effect on the quality of moral *reasoning* but that higher levels of moral reasoning are positively correlated with various types of moral behavior, such as refusing opportunities to steal, disregarding orders to harm another person, or living up to prior agreements. See Alan I. Lockwood, "The Effects of Values Clarification and Moral Development Curricula on School-Age Subjects," *Rev. of Educ. Research* 48 (1978): 325; Dennis Krebs and Alli Rosenwald, "Moral Reasoning and Moral Behavior in Conventional Adults," *Merrill-Palmer Quarterly* 23 (1977): 77. Other research has shown that certain types of people are much more desirous of living by their beliefs and do so to a much greater extent than those who have a more situation-oriented approach or who think little about ethical standards. Still other psychologists report that people who have learned to be more precise about what they believe and how their beliefs apply to real problems are more likely to act according to their

Certain professional schools can do even more than teach their students to think more carefully about difficult moral dilemmas. In faculties of business, public administration, education, and law, professors can also take an interest in the problem of how to establish environments that reinforce rather than undermine ethical behavior. The moral standards of a society are shaped not only by the character of its members but by the incentives provided by the communities in which individuals live and work. If a business sets performance standards so high that employees must resort to subterfuge in order to succeed, if government agencies invite lawlessness by failing to enforce regulations adequately, if judges devise rules that reward evasion, or if schools allow honor systems to erode from widespread cheating, even decent people may come to behave unethically. As a result, faculties that prepare students to lead organizations need to discover what factors help to create a healthy moral environment and then transmit this knowledge in their curricula. In this way they can try to teach their students now to avoid creating institutions that corrupt good character by generating pressures and temptations to mislead and manipulate others.

Rules of Conduct

Even the staunchest advocates of courses in applied ethics or professional responsibility would admit that their effects on behavior are limited and uncertain. Hence, universities need to consider the larger campus environment beyond the classroom. An obvious step in this direction is to have rules that prohibit

---

opinions. At the very least, therefore, the evidence suggests that courses in moral reasoning will have *some* beneficial effect on the conduct of *some* people *some* of the time. See generally chapters by Mark Snyder, Robert P. Abelson, and Mark P. Zanna and James M. Olson in Mark P. Zanna, E. Tory Higgins, and C. Peter Herman, *Consistency in Social Behavior*, vol. 2 of the Ontario Symposium (Hillsdale, N.J.: Lawrence Erlbaum Associates, 1982).

lying, cheating, stealing, violent behavior, interference with free expression, or other acts that break fundamental norms. Such rules not only protect the rights of everyone in the community; they also signal the importance of basic moral obligations and strengthen habits of ethical behavior.

But students do not learn to put ethical precepts into practice by rules and punishments alone. This much seems plain from looking at all of the disobedience that accompanied the stern campus discipline of the nineteenth century. If rules are truly meant to educate and not merely coerce, campus officials must bear additional principles in mind.

Although universities no longer stand in loco parentis toward their students, their purpose is always to teach and to explain. Hence, those who administer discipline should enact rules only where they have a persuasive justification and should publish the reasons for each requirement whenever the rationale is not clear. This point seems obvious, yet it is frequently overlooked. For example, in one university handbook, undergraduates are informed that "recognized organizations must maintain their local autonomy," that "no organization shall be allowed to appear on a commercially sponsored radio or television program," and that "no student resident in a University dormitory may operate a business out of his or her room." The reasons for these rules are not obvious, yet nowhere are they set forth.

Bereft of explanations to connect the rules with underlying ethical principles, such regulations can evoke a legalistic attitude in which only published rules are obeyed and students object to being punished for any conduct that is not expressly prohibited. Worse yet, as more and more prohibitions accumulate, many of them are not enforced at all by campus authorities. Not only does this permit an arbitrary use of power; it undermines the importance of rules and makes them an object of cynicism and derision.

A second requirement, which hardly needs explanation, is

that regulations must be administered fairly and consistently with penalties sufficient to make the rules credible. Most campuses satisfy this standard most of the time. But some rules, such as prohibitions against drinking alcohol or smoking marijuana, are often not enforced by proctors who object to the law or do not wish to become unpopular by reporting violations. Acts of a political nature, such as harassing speakers or occupying buildings, frequently result in only token penalties so long as no violence is done to persons or property. Still other rules are rarely invoked against certain privileged persons, a practice that has become more common as universities find themselves in strenuous competition for distinguished faculty members who bring prestige to the institution. All of these inconsistencies set a poor example for students and help to undermine respect for law.

On other occasions faculty members or administrators will seek to camouflage embarrassing incidents to avoid adverse publicity. Few institutions are free of such lapses. Some years ago, for example, local newspapers recounted the extraordinary tale of a resident in one of Harvard's teaching hospitals who had sexually assaulted several patients. Rather than discipline the culprit, or insist on appropriate psychiatric treatment, those in charge first arranged for him to leave quietly and then sent letters of recommendation to other hospitals without mentioning the circumstances of his departure. The lesson conveyed by this episode could hardly have been more unfortunate.

A final aim in maintaining discipline should be to involve students in the process of devising and administering rules. The more responsibility students can assume, the more likely they are to understand the reasons for regulations and to gain a stake in implementing them successfully. For example, no system for maintaining the right to speak on campus is likely to work well without building a strong grass-roots consensus based on a thorough understanding of the reasons for valuing free expression.

In addition to discussing rules, students can also assist in their administration and thereby gain greater commitment to basic principles of behavior and greater experience in self-government. In fact, most institutions already include students as members of judicial bodies at least for some types of offenses. An even more extensive form of student participation occurs in schools with honor codes. At Haverford, for example, under-graduates not only vote each year on whether to renew their code but take responsibility for educating freshmen about the system, sit on judicial boards to consider violations, and pledge to turn in classmates if they observe them cheating.

Perhaps the greatest benefit of honor systems is the stimulus they give students to think about their own moral responsibility and to discuss the subject among themselves. This is such an important advantage that one wonders why more colleges have not adopted an honor code of their own. Presumably, the pervasive competition for grades; the size, diversity, and imper-sonal nature of many large universities; their lack of any honor code tradition; and the widespread distaste for accusing one's classmates—all combine to curb enthusiasm for such an innova-tion. In the absence of strong student support it would surely be unwise to try to introduce a system of this kind. To try to force students against their will to turn in friends who violate the code might actually erode rather than strengthen respect for ethical standards. Still, even if students refuse to have an honor code, it is worth considering whether some equivalent can be found that will do as much to provoke serious thought about issues of moral responsibility.

Acquiring Concern for Others

Moral and social responsibility cannot develop through rules and penalties alone. They must grow out of a genuine concern for others. The best way of acquiring this concern is to experience situations in which one can appreciate the effects of one's actions on others and understand how one's own interests are affected in return. A university education does not automatically offer enough of these experiences. Often, students pursue their studies alone in competition with their peers for the grades that will give them entry to the best graduate schools and the choicest careers. Without more, such an environment can drive people apart rather than enhance their sense of responsibility to others.

This danger can be countered by extracurricular activities that bring the participants into collaborative or communal relationships—especially if someone with experience is available to offer advice and counsel when ethical challenges arise. Living together in residence halls offers an excellent opportunity for such experiences. So may athletic teams, drama clubs, orchestras, political groups, and many other activities common to most college campuses. Self-government can provide a particularly valuable experience if students are empowered to exercise responsibility over matters of genuine significance to their lives.

In graduate and professional schools, on the other hand, extracurricular activities are less numerous and the curriculum may not offer many opportunities for properly supervised collaboration. Indeed, some forms of collaboration may even be prohibited. For example, many professional schools will refuse to allow groups of students to join in writing papers because it will be impossible to grade each student's individual contribution. Rather than discourage such initiatives, faculties need to build cooperative work into the educational program and foster adequately supervised group activities of a quasi-professional nature outside the curriculum.

Of all collaborative activities, community service programs, such as tutoring underprivileged children or working in shelters for the homeless, are the most valuable, since they offer students such a vivid opportunity not only to perceive the needs of others but to act affirmatively to help people less fortunate than themselves. Such programs are all the more important today in light of the twenty-year trend among college freshmen toward valuing self-centered aspirations at the expense of more altruistic goals. To foster these activities, universities should encourage them publicly, give seed money to help them get started, and provide adequate counselling and supervision. Professional schools could even offer further incentives by giving positive weight to applications from students who have devoted substantial time and effort to endeavors of this kind.

Notwithstanding the polls indicating a rise of self-serving attitudes among entering freshmen, community service programs typically receive an enthusiastic reception from students. Following several years of encouragement, over 60 percent of all Harvard undergraduates now engage at some point during their four years in teaching children in public housing projects, staffing shelters for battered women, working with prison inmates, teaching illiterate adults to read, or acting in some other way to help people in need. Other campuses that actively promote such activities report a similar response. Community service programs need not be confined to undergraduates. In professional schools as well, law students all over the country are at work giving free legal services to the poor, medical students help staff clinics in ghetto areas, and students of education often do their practice teaching in inner-city schools. Students in schools of business or public administration could easily engage in programs of their own. For young people preparing for every profession, these experiences will often do more to build civic spirit and a lasting concern for others than any lessons learned through reading and discussion.

In recent years university administrators have begun to do more to foster community service. Approximately 225 institutions have joined a new organization, Campus Compact, to encourage such activities. Yet community service still does not receive the backing it deserves from our colleges and universities. Only a minority of campuses have sponsored programs of this kind, and only a small fraction of the student body is typically involved. Moreover, the institutions that do have programs rarely give them much support. It is sad but true that community service activities almost never receive as much experienced help and supervision as colleges offer even to their most inconsequential athletic teams.

Ethical Standards of the Institution

Universities periodically encounter ethical problems in the course of investing their stock, interacting with the surrounding community, implementing affirmative action, and engaging in other familiar activities. The way in which they address these issues will not be lost upon their students. Nothing is so likely to produce cynicism, especially among those taking courses in practical ethics, as a realization that the very institution that provides such classes shows little concern for living up to its own moral obligations.

Although the environment of the university can often seem anarchic and permissive, it helps in important ways to cause administrators and faculty members to adhere to ethical standards. Campus debate often clarifies moral choices and improves the quality of official decisions. Prevailing scholarly values emphasizing accuracy and meticulousness reinforce high standards of intellectual honesty. In an institution that relies on personal influence rather than formal power, presidents, deans, and professors must all behave ethically in order to gain and retain respect. If nothing else, campus authorities know that they work in something akin to a goldfish bowl and hence are not likely to utter convenient untruths or cut ethical corners to achieve their ends.

Not all the features of the modern university, however, serve to buttress high standards of morality. As we have seen, the keen competition for prestige among American universities can lead institutions to condone or cover up activities where disclosure could cause unfavorable publicity or induce famous professors to leave. In addition, however hard it tries, a modern university cannot avoid embarrassing mistakes and moral lapses. Hundreds of people make hundreds of decisions each day. Most of these decisions are made with considerable independence and often under pressure of time. In such circumstances, deplorable incidents are bound to occur. One could try to reduce their number by imposing more rules and review procedures. But controls of this kind would only increase red tape and stifle the independent judgment essential to an institution that seeks to be creative and personal rather than cumbersome and bureaucratic.

Apart from the inevitable mistakes, problems of communication often make the performance of a university seem worse than it actually is. In some instances, officials are bound by decency not to disclose all the facts, even when it is embarrassing to keep silent. Most universities will not reveal the reasons why a popular athlete has been suspended, nor will a faculty accused of failing to promote a popular young professor for political, racial, or gender reasons disclose the confidential judgments from outside experts on the candidate's published scholarly work that actually accounted for the decision.

Even when officials are free to publicize the facts, they may have difficulty establishing their credibility or having their message understood. Universities are large established organizations in a society that lacks confidence in such institutions and their leaders. Surrounded by skeptics and beset by demands for money to finance a long list of programs, the most conscientious educators can easily appear to be influenced more by financial needs than by ethical considerations. These perceptions are frequently enhanced by the fact that campus officials must convey their decisions to students through the prism of the media. When controversial issues arise, there will be no dearth of critics willing to supply unsavory reasons to explain the administration's actions. Newspaper reporters will be quick to publicize these claims, since stories suggesting intrigue and evil motives make more interesting reading than dry recitations of fact.* In such an environment the most principled university president may be regarded much as the fabled administrator about whom it was said: "If he were taken to the hospital to have his conscience removed, one would have to classify it as a minor operation."

The tortured issue of whether to invest in firms operating in South Africa offers a particularly vivid example of the hazards that arise in trying to demonstrate a sincere commitment to high ethical standards. The problems of South Africa are too difficult and too inflammatory to escape bitter controversy. Whatever the institution does will antagonize some segment of the greater university community. Student activists will claim that any official who opposes divestment is insensitive to the injustices of apartheid while conservative alumni insist that selling stock is only an empty and expensive gesture to appease campus radicals. In such circumstances, no course of action will satisfy everyone or preserve the administration from charges of moral dereliction.

The record of higher education in responding to this challenge has been decidedly mixed. Several universities holding widely divergent views on divestment have made conscientious efforts to listen to opinions from all quarters, to deliberate carefully, to

---

*This tendency may explain why surveys consistently show that people's opinions gained from direct experience, such as feelings about their *own* high school, their *own* doctor, or their *own* congressman, are much more favorable than their views about categories, such as schools, the medical profession, or the Congress, where their impressions of these institutions derive from media accounts.

discuss the subject openly, and to publish detailed reasons for their policies. Other institutions on both sides of the issue have performed less creditably, either refusing to discuss the matter at all or offering confused explanations for their actions. For example, consider the following announcement by a board of trustees following prolonged campus protest.

> The University [will] divest all its holdings in companies with operations in South Africa.
>
> Nothing in this resolution shall be deemed to direct the sales of holdings at an imprudent time . . .
>
> The Board of Trustees joins the Joint Investments Committee in reasserting:
>
> (1) Its belief in the fundamental importance of political neutrality in maintaining the academic freedom of the university; and
> (2) Its belief that the companies operating in South Africa in which the University owns stock have not only met the highest standards of the Sullivan Principles, but have made a positive contribution to the current and future well-being of the Black People of South Africa.

What can students make of this statement except that the university is determined not to offend anyone?*

---

*Questionable results have also occurred in other institutions, both those that have divested totally and those that have not. Universities with large portfolios have often explained their refusal to divest without speaking frankly about their unwillingness to risk substantial losses in their endowment even though such risks must obviously have played a significant role in the final decision. On the other hand, announcements of "total divestment" have sometimes turned out in practice not to apply to large index funds holding stocks of firms doing business in South Africa or to foreign companies with extensive South African operations. In all these cases, the administration's action can only provoke cynicism once the truth of the matter becomes known.

Fortunately, most ethical issues on campus are not as inflammatory as South Africa, so that it is easier to discuss them objectively. As a result, despite the unavoidable moral lapses, the distortions, and the passionate disagreements, if officials take pains to consider ethical issues carefully, to explain their actions clearly, and to rebut unfounded attacks on their position, they have a decent chance of persuading most people that they are serious in their concern for ethical issues and their desire to act reasonably and fairly. On occasion, even this goal may seem very hard to achieve. Yet the alternative is surely far worse. If universities are slow to explain their policies and careless in replying to critics, they will only seem morally callous and leave themselves vulnerable to those who seek to discredit their actions and charge them with venal and sinister motives. In such an atmosphere, any effort to foster ethical standards will soon fall victim to cynicism and distrust.

The Institutional Environment

The examples universities set through their official policies are but a few of the innumerable messages bearing ethical content that pass through the campus community. Coaches periodically grapple with moral issues in full view of their players as they strive to resolve conflicts between winning and playing by the rules. Financial aid officers must cope with students who misrepresent their family assets. Proctors have to respond to petty acts of discrimination against black, women, or gay undergraduates. By the way they treat individual students and staff, professors signal to their students whether important people need have concern for others or whether they can get ahead with little regard for anyone save themselves. By the questions they contain, even application forms suggest the importance professional schools attach to matters of character as opposed to matters of intellect.

To create an ethical environment, universities must try to make these implicit messages affirm rather than undermine basic moral values. But university officials are hampered in this effort by the fact that they possess so little authority over professors, who exercise the greatest influence over the attitudes of students. The strong commitment to academic freedom precludes an administration from trying to influence the views of faculty members, even if a professor utters bizarre ethical opinions or openly disparages moral values. In addition, as we have seen, universities have largely abandoned the attempt to pick professors on the basis of their moral character. The prospects for changing this practice are slight.* From a practical standpoint, it is very difficult to evaluate something as elusive as "character" or to obtain enough evidence about a prospective faculty member to make a comprehensive, well-substantiated appraisal. At best, a university can merely ask how conscientiously candidates fulfill their basic obligations to students and investigate any indications of professional impropriety or of flagrant misconduct in a candidate's personal life.

Fortunately, however, most faculty members do set high standards of probity, conscientiousness, and service to others. Moreover, though professors will occasionally behave in improper ways, students can learn from bad examples as well as good ones. Indeed, a morally perfect environment might be a

---

*Since it is so difficult to assess character, faculties would resist attempts to alter this practice, fearing that academic quality might suffer and that "character" could too easily become a cloak for discriminating against candidates who come from different ethnic groups or hold controversial views. After all, even Charles W. Eliot, greatest of all Harvard presidents, was said to have turned down a prospective faculty member on the ground that "his wife is a she-devil" (Ephraim Emerton, "Personal Recollections of Charles William Eliot," *Harvard Graduates' Magazine* (1924), n. 11 at p. 350). Besides, in today's highly competitive atmosphere, few universities would agree to forgo appointing a brilliant scientist or a distinguished scholar on grounds of character save in clear-cut cases.

poor preparation for the real world. What is truly destructive is not the fact that immoral acts occur but the willingness of an administration to overlook them. This is a matter that does lie within the university's control. Even the tenets of academic freedom do not prevent an administration from holding the faculty to appropriate rules regarding sexual harassment, conflicts of interest, excessive consulting, and other forms of misconduct.

Faculties can also discuss the responsibilities of their office among themselves and thus develop norms and expectations that exert a powerful effect on individual colleagues. Such discussions are already common with regard to problems such as consulting or conflicts of interest, though even here there is often a reluctance to institute reporting requirements and other methods to ensure that agreed-upon norms are observed. Much less frequent are efforts to clarify the faculty's responsibilities as teachers—to return student work promptly with adequate comment, to contribute sufficiently to student advising, to supervise teaching fellows adequately, and to give proper guidance to graduate students writing theses. As a result, while most professors may perform their duties conscientiously, some do not. The willingness to tolerate such behavior can only arouse a suspicion among students that people in positions of power do not necessarily have to be scrupulous in living up to their responsibilities toward others.

The administration could likewise do more by preparing proctors, student advisors, administrative deans, and financial aid officers to respond more perceptively to the issues of honesty, promise-keeping, and deception that periodically arise in working with students. Intercollegiate sports offer a particularly apt example, since coaches can have such a powerful effect on their players and because varsity athletics constantly present sharp conflicts between ends and means. Alas, few universities with big-time programs have done much to prepare their coaches to address moral problems, or even to convince them that winning is not the most important criterion for judging their performance. Of course, many coaches do manage to set a good ethical example for their teams. But many others have involved their players in a long list of dubious maneuvers to gain a competitive edge: allowing unauthorized scrimmages to occur, encouraging an excessively violent style of play, keeping star athletes eligible even when they misbehave, committing petty recruiting violations. The persistence of these transgressions and the willingness of campus authorities to condone them send a damaging message to students about just how important ethical standards are when they conflict with intense desires to succeed.

The Program Reconsidered

These, then, are the elements of a comprehensive program of moral education: offering courses in applied ethics at the college and professional school level, discussing rules of conduct with students and administering them fairly, building strong programs of community service, demonstrating high ethical standards in dealing with moral issues facing the university, and, finally, being more alert to the countless signals that institutions send to students and trying to make these messages support rather than undermine basic norms.

This account should reassure those who fear that any effort to strengthen ethical standards will turn out to be a form of indoctrination. Nothing I have mentioned should compromise the university's obligation to respect the freedom of every student to express any opinion or entertain any view on moral as well as political, social, and aesthetic questions. That is why particular religious doctrines, however important they may be in guiding the ethical beliefs of individual students, can never be used by a secular university as the basis for its program of moral education. What the institution *can* do is to offer arguments and encouragement of various kinds to persuade students to adhere to certain basic norms. These norms—honesty, nonviolence, promise-keeping, respect for property and other legitimate interests—are all so fundamental and so universal that they have proved essential to virtually every civilized society. As a result, institutional efforts encouraging students to act according to these precepts should not give justifiable offense to any campus group. After all, would any sensible person urge university officials *not* to speak out in favor of honesty and free speech, *not* to advocate community service, *not* to strive for a high ethical standard in setting institutional policy, *not* to adopt reasonable disciplinary rules against violence, cheating, or plagiarism?

The efforts described, therefore, hardly amount to indoctrination, nor are they morally neutral to the point of breeding ethical relativism. But will they do any good? A university is only one institution among many that affect students' lives. It offers an experience late in youth when ideas and values are more developed and students less open to adult advice than in earlier years. It competes with television, motion pictures, and the tumult of an outside world replete with scandals and lurid exposés. With its commitment to intellectual freedom and diversity, a university even lacks the power to bring a consistent, coordinated influence to bear on those who live and work within its walls. For many students, its efforts to communicate on moral questions will be all but lost amid the distractions of the host of organizations and extracurricular activities that fill the typical campus.

Despite these limitations, the years of college and professional school still represent an important stage in the development of most young people. In graduate schools of law, business, medicine, and the like, students form a sense of what kind of a professional they wish to be—what skills and attitudes matter most and how they can adapt their values to the special circumstances and challenges of their calling. In college, freshmen arrive, often free from family influence for the first time, to think about their lives in new and different ways. As many observers have noted, this experience frequently leads students to discard their simple moral codes in favor of new sets of values. The new values are often the product of considerable thought and intro- spection and are typically built upon some notion of the recipro- cal obligations human beings need to observe toward one an- other in order to form a viable community. In Carol Gilligan's words, "Moral development in the college years thus centers on the shift from moral ideology to ethical responsibility."[4]

As students search to define their ethical responsibilities, the university can play an important role. Its usefulness comes in part from its capacity to instill a greater respect for facts and a greater ability to reason carefully about complicated problems. Equally valuable is its diverse community populated by students and faculty with many different backgrounds and points of view. Such an environment teaches tolerance, a respect for differing values, a recognition of the complexity of human problems. In so doing, it prepares students well for the real world and helps a perceptive person to acquire a moral understanding far richer and more firmly rooted in the intricacies of modern life than simpler dogmas nurtured in more homogeneous, more arti- ficially controlled environments.

These advantages, however, are not sufficient to insure a sound moral education. Indeed, they carry substantial risks that need to be countered by a serious effort on the part of the university. Precisely because its community is so diverse, set in a society so divided and confused over its values, a university that pays little attention to moral development may find that many of its students grow bewildered, convinced that ethical dilemmas are insoluble and should be regarded as matters of personal opinion beyond external judgment or careful analysis.

Nothing could be more unfortunate or more unnecessary.

Although moral issues sometimes lack convincing answers, that is not necessarily the case. Besides, universities should be the last institutions to discourage a belief in the value of reasoned argument and carefully considered evidence in analyzing even the hardest human problems. And universities should be among the first to reaffirm the importance of basic norms such as honesty, promise-keeping, free expression, and helping others, for these are not only principles essential to civilized society; they are values on which all learning and discovery ultimately depend. There is nothing odd or inappropriate, therefore, for a university to use them as the foundation for a determined program to help students develop a strong set of moral standards. On the contrary, the failure to do so threatens to convey a message that neither these values nor the effort to live up to them are of great importance or common concern. This message is not only unworthy of the academy; it is likely in the atmosphere of a university to leave students morally confused and unable to acquire strong ethical convictions of their own.

The Record of Progress

Surveying the efforts currently made to help students acquire a stronger sense of moral and civic responsibility, one cannot say that higher education as a whole pays adequate attention to the issue. Some efforts are being made on every campus, and a number of religious institutions and small independent colleges actually devote much time and energy to the task. More often, however, and especially in large universities, the subject is still not treated as a serious responsibility worthy of sustained discussion and determined action by the faculty and administration.

Even courses in applied ethics, despite their recent vogue, have not yet come to occupy a secure and central place within the curriculum. Whereas most medical schools offer at least one course in medical ethics, such offerings typically reach only a minority of the student body. A survey in 1982 covering hundreds of business programs, graduate and undergraduate, revealed that only 40 percent offered any instruction at all in ethics.5 One-third of all graduate schools of public administration offered no course in ethics, and only one-third mandated such instruction for all students.6 Even in law schools, where courses on professional responsibility are virtually compulsory, thanks to the American Bar Association, surveys report that most students regard them as less rigorous and less ably taught than other offerings in the curriculum.7

Other aspects of moral and civic education are in an equally imperfect condition. It is safe to say that most universities do not enlist a majority of their students in adequately supervised programs of community service, do not carefully explain the reasons for their rules of conduct, do not engage their students in shaping and administering such rules, and do not make a sustained, serious effort to explain their actions in addressing the moral questions that regularly confront the institution.

There are many reasons for this neglect. Because of its checkered history, its religious overtones, its aroma of indoctrination, moral education is an awkward topic that is all too easy to ignore. That may be why faculties often resort to spurious arguments (e.g., "by the time you come to business school, you either have ethics or you don't") to justify their disregard of the subject. A serious program of moral education is also quite burdensome. Amid the hectic pace of campus life, it grows harder every year for presidents, deans, and other administrators to find the time and energy to mount the necessary courses, organize ambitious community service programs, and openly discuss the various disciplinary rules and ethical issues that continually arise on campus.

These problems could all be overcome, of course, if the incentives to do so were sufficiently strong. As we have seen, the mounting concern over ethical problems in society has already helped to bring forth a profusion of courses in practical ethics. But the demands of the outside world are not yet strong enough to permit these offerings to achieve a secure place in the curriculum. No student receives a higher salary or a better job because he has worked hard at courses in moral reasoning. Most foundations and corporations are still reluctant to fund programs in applied ethics, because they either have doubts about the intellectual rigor of the field or are fearful of arousing controversy in their boards over ideological issues. Within the academy, applied ethics is still not a fully accepted field within philosophy, nor can an institution aspire to greater prestige by mounting a strong program in the subject. While moral dilemmas and issues of social responsibility are often discussed in respectable academic journals, they are hardly the stuff on which to build a strong scholarly reputation. In such an environment, the effort to strengthen ethical standards and civic virtues—though greater than it was—continues to be a precarious and marginal enterprise.

Although the future of moral education remains in doubt, the proper course for universities to take seems clear enough. With their classes, residence halls, extracurricular activities, and counseling services, colleges and universities create a world that dominates the lives and thoughts of countless young people during years in which their character and values are still being formed. Within this environment, students must get help from their universities in developing moral standards and civic responsibilities or they are unlikely to get much help at all. In these circumstances, even if presidents are overburdened and professors feel untrained for the task, they have no choice but to try to assist their students in learning how to lead ethical, socially responsible lives. One can appreciate the difficulty of the enterprise and understand if progress is slow. What is harder to forgive is a refusal even to recognize the problem or to acknowledge a duty to work at it conscientiously.

CHAPTER FIVE

Prospects for Reform

———

A merican universities are a many-splendored creation. Their colleges offer an experience that countless graduates look back upon with unusual warmth and appreciation. Their doctoral programs attract outstanding students from every corner of the globe. Their professional schools are widely emulated abroad, while the achievements of their laboratories and the quality of their scholarship have come to be universally admired.

As their eminence has grown, universities have steadily become more important to a nation increasingly dependent on new discoveries, expert knowledge, and highly trained personnel. Yet, this newfound influence has proved to be a mixed blessing. It has brought forth vast sums of money from government agencies, corporations, and foundations along with greater visibility and excitement for professors hurrying to counsel heads of state or busily offering opinions to the media. But it has also produced in Oscar Handlin's words "a genuine concern that a troubled universe can no longer afford the luxury of pursuits confined to an ivory tower so that scholarship has to prove its worth not on its own terms, but by service to the nation and the world."[1] Such an environment provokes troubling questions. How to engage more closely with the outside world and not succumb to its blandishments, its distractions, its corrupting entanglements? How to serve society's immediate needs and not neglect the more profound obligation that every institution of learning owes to civilization to renew its culture, interpret its past, and expand our understanding of the human condition?

Whatever the difficulty and however risky the enterprise, there is no avoiding the attempt to combine efforts to serve the outside world with less utilitarian intellectual pursuits. So long as universities depend on society for their existence and so long as society requires the education and expertise that these institutions can uniquely supply, the academy has no choice but to do its part to meet the nation's legitimate needs. The obligation can only grow heavier at a time like the present when America's efforts to couple prosperity with security and opportunity for all seem beset by such formidable problems.

How well do our universities perform in addressing the nation's agenda? In many respects, the record is excellent. When society recognizes a need that can be satisfied through advanced education or research *and* when sufficient funds are available to pay the cost, American universities respond in exemplary fashion. Exploring the basic sciences, investigating disease, or educating scientists, physicians, business executives, and corporate lawyers, our universities probably succeed more fully than their counterparts anywhere in the world. The competition among 3,000 colleges and hundreds of universities, all striving to attract better students and professors and to enhance their reputations, unleashes exceptional energy and initiative in pursuit of better programs of research and education. In contrast, other systems of higher education, which tend to be centrally controlled and disinclined to compete, are slower to depart from tradition and to embark on new initiatives.

In short, our universities excel in pursuing the easier opportunities where established academic and social priorities coincide. On the other hand, when social needs are not clearly recognized and backed by adequate financial support, higher education has often failed to respond as effectively as it might, even to some of the most important challenges facing America. Armed with the security of tenure and the time to study the world with care, professors would appear to have a unique opportunity to act as society's scouts to signal impending problems long before they are visible to others. Yet rarely have members of the academy succeeded in discovering emerging issues and bringing them vividly to the attention of the public. What Rachel Carson did for risks to the environment, Ralph Nader for consumer protection, Michael Harrington for problems of poverty, Betty Friedan for women's rights, they did as independent critics, not as members of a faculty. Even the seminal work on the plight of blacks in America was written by a Swedish social scientist, not by a member of an American university.

After a major social problem has been recognized, universities will usually continue to respond weakly unless outside support is available and the subjects involved command prestige in academic circles. These limitations have hampered efforts to address many of the most critical challenges to the nation. If universities were fully responsive to society's needs, business schools would give a high priority to the management of technology and product design, the organization and motivation of employees, and the problems of doing business abroad. Engineering schools would offer strong programs in manufacturing and design. Universities would strive to maintain schools of education and public service of a quality and strength commensurate with the importance of these fields of activity. Urban institutes, schools of social work, and public policy faculties would produce a quantity and quality of research on poverty and its associated problems more in keeping with the urgency of these issues. Colleges and universities would do their best to promote ethical standards and civic responsibility through their curricula, rules of conduct, community service programs, and all the other policies and practices that communicate the values of the institution to its students.

With few exceptions, universities have not pursued these opportunities vigorously or fully acknowledged their importance. True, progress has begun to occur in some areas after strong expressions of public concern. Management schools have added courses on international business and technology, engineering faculties have strengthened their programs in manufacturing and design, and colleges and professional schools are offering more courses in applied ethics. Even in these cases, however, the effort is not yet equal to the need, and the belated response means that the effects will not be felt for a considerable time.

In other areas, the situation is still less promising. Despite universal concern over the plight of our public schools, there is no indication that faculties of education are rising in importance or quality. Only a few schools of public administration are improving significantly, notwithstanding the general dissatisfaction over the effectiveness of government at all levels. Faculties of social work and human services continue to languish in the face of ever more dismaying problems of poor people and blighted urban communities.

The Role of Leadership

Can anything be done to help universities respond more quickly and fully to society's needs? Some would argue that there is no cure for the status quo that would not be worse than the disease. Although universities could doubtless do more to help society overcome its difficulties, no one can be sure what patterns of teaching and research are truly ideal. Hence, the interplay between individual teachers and scholars pursuing their intellectual interests and a diverse group of funding sources may provide a marketplace of sorts that yields results better than any substitute that human ingenuity could devise. Individual professors can do their best work only insofar as they are allowed to choose the subjects that interest them the most and seem most susceptible to systematic thought and investigation. The presence of many autonomous funding sources permits scholars to search for opportunities that strike them as promising and important while minimizing the risk that any deserving subject will go unrecognized and unsupported. The results of this process may not be perfect. But will they not be far superior to any system that fixes priorities to fit a set of predetermined social needs?

Such arguments make a convincing case against any solution that relies on central planning to set the agenda for higher education. It is the penchant for such planning, after all, that has made most other systems of higher education even less responsible and effective than our own. Nevertheless, there are steps far short of centralized control that could help universities respond better to society's needs.

The most obvious key to progress is effective leadership from those who preside over universities and their faculties. Presidents and deans are in a better position than anyone to perceive the social problems that will benefit most from education and research and to encourage faculty members to respond accordingly. No one else can so readily secure the necessary funds, either by reallocating internal resources or by persuading outside sources that the cause is worth supporting. Granted, such leadership will have to be resourceful and tenacious in order to succeed. Still, examples are not difficult to find. Let me illustrate by citing two examples taken from my own university.

The first illustration comes from the School of Education. The national shortage of qualified teachers of science and mathematics has become a serious problem, especially as the economy becomes more technologically sophisticated and demands greater numbers of skilled employees working with highly complex equipment. At first glance, the problem appears insoluble, since college graduates with training in math and science can command much higher salaries in industry than they can hope to obtain by teaching school. Nevertheless, Dean Patricia Graham conceived of a way to escape this dilemma. She urged the creation of a one-year mid-career course for middle-aged professionals with math and science backgrounds, such as military officers and industrial engineers, who wished to spend the last ten to twenty years of their active career teaching children in the public schools. Since many of these professionals were eligible for half-pensions which could be added to their teacher's salaries, the financial barriers were not insuperable. Within four years, applications exceeded 100 for only 25 places. By itself, of course, a program of this size could hardly make a dent on the national problem. But the enterprise soon attracted attention, and similar initiatives began to develop in other universities. By 1988, over two dozen programs were in operation; together, they currently graduate hundreds of qualified math and science teachers every year.

The second example involves the transformation of a faculty of public administration. In the late 1960s, four Harvard professors with extensive government experience became concerned about the effectiveness of government and the quality of its officials. Convinced that they could devise better methods to prepare students for government service, they created a small pilot program emphasizing techniques of policy analysis that were beginning to have wide application in Washington. The new curriculum showed that it was possible to mount courses for aspiring public officials that were as useful and as rigorous as those of the more established professional schools. Getting financial support proved more difficult. After several frustrating years, however, an unusually resourceful dean, Graham Allison, began to find the funds required to build needed facilities and expand the faculty. Enrollments grew and executive programs were added for newly elected mayors and congressmen, national security officers, senior civil servants, state and local officials, and many more. Though building a school required hard work and called for forms of scholarship not wholly suitable for advancement in the established disciplines, outstanding young Ph.D.'s were persuaded to take a chance and cast their lot with this new academic venture. Today, the John F. Kennedy School of Government has a full-time faculty of seventy, an endowment of $120 million, and a student body comparable in quality to that of older, more established faculties, such as law and business.

Similar opportunities for leadership exist in the field of moral education as well. It does not take prohibitive sums of money to mount successful courses in professional ethics, develop community service programs, or set a high example of institutional behavior to affirm the importance of ethical standards. Rather, the challenge is to muster the cooperation of faculty and staff by persuading them to recognize the need to help students develop a stronger commitment to ethical standards and a stronger sense of responsibility to others. Individual colleges, such as Haverford and Notre Dame, have shown how far one can succeed in this endeavor by sustained, determined effort. On a national scale, philosopher Daniel Callahan and psychologist Willard Gaylin have played a major role in building the entire field of applied ethics through the work of the Hastings Institute. By supporting and publishing research in medical ethics and by organizing countless meetings and colloquia, the Institute managed single-handedly to create a community of interested scholars throughout the country.

Of course, leadership has its limits, especially when the task at hand is large enough to require the transformation of an entire faculty or professional school. The most enthusiastic president cannot conjure up tens of millions of dollars to strengthen areas of work that command no interest in the outside world. Provosts cannot build great faculties in subjects where the supply of outstanding scholars is very small, nor can deans attract large numbers of talented students into fields where pay and prestige are less than adequate. Still, effective leadership can usually make a difference great enough to make the effort worthwhile, especially when the obstacles are not too severe. By reallocating internal resources or by determined fund-raising, presidents and deans can develop robust programs of international business, production engineering and design, or poverty research. With persuasion and modest financial help, faculties can be induced to improve their offerings in other languages and cultures or to build programs of moral education. With exceptional skill and dedication, it is even possible to build a strong school of public policy or education.

The key question is whether such leadership will emerge. As costs continue to rise and government spending lags, university presidents must devote more time to lobbying public officials and funds. Meanwhile, faculties have extended their control over academic policies, relegating presidents even more to administrative and external duties. Quoting from a survey of 700 university presidents, William Bennett reported in 1984 that less than 2 percent "described themselves as playing a major role in academic affairs."[2] These trends all serve to weaken the tenuous links that connect the needs of society with the priorities of the university. Even if presidents do play a stronger role in shaping academic programs, they will also have to swim against the tide in order to launch serious efforts to address the practical problems of society. For though competition drives university leaders and their faculties to intense and unremitting effort, what competition rewards is chiefly success in fields that command conventional academic prestige rather than success in responding to important social needs. The media, with their primitive ratings and polls, only serve to strengthen this tendency. All in all, therefore, though it is still possible to lead a university toward higher levels of social responsibility, the obstacles are substantial and seem to be growing all the time.

The Role of Outside Agencies

Because of the forces inhibiting leadership, outside groups need to lend a hand to stimulate and support creative responses to national problems. This suggestion may strike some university colleagues as heretical, even disloyal. The academy, like every successful professional group, does not relish the thought of outside interference. If carried too far, such pressure is usually counterproductive. Only professors can judge what subjects lend themselves to effective teaching and research, and efforts to push them against their will are bound to end in failure. No good book was ever written on command, nor can good teaching occur under duress. And yet, conceding this, the fact remains that left entirely to their own devices, academic communities are no less prone than other professional organizations to slip unconsciously into complacent habits, inward-looking standards of quality, self-serving canons of behavior. To counter these tendencies, there will always be a need to engage the outside world in a lively, continuing debate over the university's social responsibilities.

Trustees. Governing boards offer one promising possibility. It is their special responsibility to choose university presidents and hence to define their proper role. In recent decades, as we have seen, that role has been reshaped to emphasize fund-raising and external affairs, leaving academic matters increasingly in the hands of the faculty. The result has been to diminish the university's capacity to set clear priorities that reconcile the standards of the academy with the legitimate needs of the larger society. If this deficiency is to be overcome and a proper place for leadership restored, the trustees must make clear that they want the president to exercise such responsibility and then support their chosen nominee in carrying out that mandate.

Trustees can also take the initiative in asking university leaders what their institutions are doing to address important social issues that call for programs of education and research. At present, so far as I am aware, few boards acknowledge this responsibility, let alone pursue it in any systematic fashion. Typically, trustees spend their time listening passively to reports from the administration, discussing matters of finance and administration, or helping to raise money. Yet there is no reason to limit their role in this fashion. Trustees are supposed to serve as links between the university and the outside world. Their function is not merely to interpret and justify the university to the larger society but to convey the legitimate needs of that society to the institutions they serve and to inquire whether more imaginative, more effective responses should be forthcoming.

In carrying out this task, of course, a board must be careful not to try to impose its views on the university. Insensitive trustees could unwittingly press universities to take on inappropriate tasks or slight the other important functions they serve. But exercising care is one thing and doing nothing to represent society's needs is quite another. By posing questions and asking the administration how it plans to respond to particular problems in society, a board of trustees could induce university leaders to accept greater social responsibility. Having done so, individual trustees could even go further and help persuade outside funding sources to support creative initiatives along these lines.

Professions. Practitioners are another group that could exercise a constructive influence on professional schools, whether as members of alumni associations or visiting committees, potential donors, or employers of graduating students. In all of these guises, practitioners should be able to communicate the emerging needs of their professions to faculties and deans. Of course, it is always possible to use this influence for petty purposes by trying to turn professional schools into trade schools that emphasize skills training and neglect research. But faculties in established universities are quite adept at resisting this sort of interference, so much so that the danger has rarely materialized. Much more often, practicing professionals have acted passively, unable or unwilling to communicate any coherent view of the needs of their calling.

In this regard, corporate executives have been particularly reticent. There is scant evidence throughout the 1970s or early 1980s that business leaders actively urged management faculties to pay closer attention to subjects such as doing business abroad, employee motivation, manufacturing, or the effective use of technology. Instead, most company officials have shown little interest in the content of the education provided by business schools. As donors, they have given to obtain personal recognition or to express loyalty to their alma mater. As employers, they have looked for the smartest students available with little apparent concern for the type of training they have received. Ironically, by acting in this fashion corporate recruiters have behaved just as Marxist economists always claimed they would, treating business schools more as sorting devices to classify talent than as institutions with an important educational mission. With so little countervailing pressure from the profession, faculties have felt free to pursue the rewards of academic prestige by emphasizing the teaching and scholarship favored by their parent disciplines with scant regard for their relevance to the real world of business.

Government officials have likewise done little to help develop stronger programs for preparing public servants. They have shown almost no interest in hiring students with a broad education in public administration, preferring instead to recruit accountants, engineers, and other specialists with skills needed for their first jobs. While government agencies may have to hire specialists to fill a host of positions, they also need executives with broad management ability. In practice, however, they have paid much less attention than corporations to nurturing these administrative skills and perspectives through programs of career development. In particular, they have given little encouragement to mid-career executive training of the kind that has proven so successful for private firms.

Professional associations have similarly failed to exert a constructive influence over the preparation of teachers. For many years, schools of education were left to devise their own programs without much outside interference. During the 1960s, state governments, foundations, and the National Education Association (NEA) all began to assert more authority. To a large extent, however, the NEA appeared to be motivated not by any vision of better teacher education but by a desire to expand its power. Thus, its substantive demands were mostly those of a self-serving guild—e.g., "support inclusion of instruction in . . . the values, ethics, responsibilities, and structure of professional teachers organizations," or "support the teaching of methods courses by teachers currently employed in elementary and secondary schools."[3]

In the 1980s, state governors and legislators began to enter the field aggressively, supported by business interests concerned over the need to compete more effectively abroad. Dozens of bills emanated from state capitols setting minimum standards for admission into teacher education programs, regulating curricula, and tightening requirements for certification. These laws were often enacted with little input from the teaching profession and soon encountered widespread criticism from independent sources. In view of this opposition, policy is shifting away from detailed state regulation toward the establishment of standards for teacher certification by a board heavy with teaching professionals. It is still too soon to tell whether this latest reform will provide a serviceable vehicle for responsible professional opinion. What does seem clear is that the teaching profession has done very little until now to help bring about improved programs of preparation.

Foundations. In addition to trustees and professionals, another group that could give a useful stimulus for reform are the agencies that fund universities, especially private foundations. Foundations, after all, are designed to encourage efforts by universities and other organizations to address important problems of society. By looking for creative initiatives, neglected areas of work, important problems that have fallen out of fashion, they can foster experimentation and supplement the efforts of government in highly valuable ways.

Much more than trustees and professionals, foundations have succeeded in providing a catalyst for constructive work on the part of higher education. Yet even they do not always exert their influence as effectively as they might. For example, their officials rarely seem to consult with universities until after their priorities have been set. As a result, not only do academic officers have no chance to express their views on how their universities could contribute to important social problems; foundations miss a valuable opportunity to encourage university leaders to think hard about how their institutions could play a more effective role.

Once their programs are launched, foundation officials seldom receive much feedback on how wisely they have acted in choosing their agenda. They are less inclined to ask for a critique of their priorities than to assess how well each of their grantees has performed. Quite naturally, the beneficiaries of their largesse are reluctant to criticize unless they are strongly urged to do so. As a result, there is little opportunity for foundations to learn from experience in order to make wiser choices in the future.

Whether for these or other reasons, foundations have done much less than they might to encourage universities to respond creatively to the range of problems discussed in these pages. That, at least, is the conclusion reached by those who have studied organized philanthropy most closely.* This verdict is borne out by the actions of foundations toward several of the needs identified in these chapters.

With respect to business schools, for example, Ford and Rockefeller sponsored reports in the late 1950s that were influential in persuading faculties to make management curricula more rigorous and to place more emphasis on research.4 But neither they nor other foundations ever returned to this subject to consider whether the pendulum they helped into motion might have swung too far. As a result, they did little or nothing during the 1960s and 1970s to encourage business schools to turn their attention to manufacturing, the management of technology, and other subjects bearing on the competitiveness of American business.

In the field of public policy and administration, foundations have also done relatively little to help universities develop better programs to prepare students for government service. An op-

---

*Waldemar Nielsen, for example, after calling particular attention to the issues of war and peace, competitiveness, and "the emerging crisis of the overburdened and underperforming welfare state," goes on to conclude: "With the exception of a splendid minority, our largest foundations are not even attempting to grapple directly with the major and most threatening problems confronting the nation and the world at the present time." *The Golden Donors* (New York: E. P. Dutton, 1985), p. 425.

portune moment presented itself in the 1970s when several universities launched new schools of public policy emphasizing methods of policy analysis developed in the postwar period. Although it was clear that the field of public administration represented a glaring weakness in American professional education and that the need for better-trained public officials was substantial, foundations gave only modest temporary support and refused to grant any endowment funds whatsoever.

The failure to play a more active, supportive role in the face of such an important need points to a deeper problem in the policies of most philanthropic institutions. By and large, foundation officials concentrate on funding programs of research and education that further goals important to other groups in the society. They rarely offer permanent funding to strengthen the academic institutions that are responsible for mounting such programs. In the case of well-established faculties, such as law, business, or medicine, this policy works well enough, since these schools have alumni and other donors to whom they can turn for permanent support. But in the case of schools of education and public administration, there are no affluent alumni bodies. As a result, a policy of making only short-term grants tends to perpetuate weakness. Rather than helping to build strong institutions that could improve the quality of education or government, foundations force these faculties into a hand-to-mouth existence, endlessly seeking new projects that funding agencies will support in order to help defray the salaries and stipends of professors and graduate students.

Foundation support has been disappointing in yet another way. Because societal problems, such as education, poverty and public policy, are characteristically vast and difficult, they require sustained funding over a long period of time. Ideally, therefore, foundations should behave in a manner countercyclical to government by taking special care to support important fields of work during times when they are neglected by public officials. In the case of education and poverty, quite the opposite has occurred. Foundations were active in supporting poverty research and schools of education in the 1960s and early 1970s, when government was also heavily involved. In the 1980s, when government research budgets declined by 50 percent or more for education and poverty-related subjects, private philanthropy did not act to minimize the damage. Indeed, major foundations actually cut back their support for educational research, and this at a time when the nation was more concerned than ever with the meager achievements of students in the public schools.

Had foundations offered endowment funds and given consistent research support through the years, they could have helped to build half a dozen first-rate schools of education and an equal number of excellent poverty centers and schools of social work and human service, all for a relatively modest investment. As it is, little progress of this sort has occurred. Over the past quarter century, therefore, organized philanthropy has done much less than it should to encourage universities to respond creatively to two of our most important domestic problems--the failure of American public education and the crisis of the urban underclass.

Government. Of all the outside forces that can affect the behavior of universities the greatest by far is the federal government. Only Washington can perceive the full sweep of problems facing our society. And only Washington commands resources on a scale sufficient to alter the priorities of all higher education.

In science, the federal government has generally used its influence in an enlightened manner to develop a large and successful research effort. True, the record has not been perfect. Because responsibility for research is divided among several agencies, there is no comprehensive review of major, cross-cutting objectives, such as maintaining the basic research infra-structure or developing a larger corps of scientists and engineers from America's youth. At times, politics enters in, as in the recent practice of earmarking money for facilities to designated institutions favored by particular legislators. On the whole, however, Congress has maintained the sustained flow of funds needed to build a first-rate scientific capability, while the Na-tional Institutes of Health, the National Science Foundation, and the Defense Department have all done a workmanlike job of supporting research according to its scientific merits.

In the social sciences, on the other hand, there is no real public consensus on the value of research and advanced education so that such work is far more vulnerable to partisan political pres-sures. As a consequence, the government has been much less successful in developing strong programs of research and train-ing than it has been for most of the sciences. In some fields, such as poverty and education, funding has fluctuated too widely to build as strong a research enterprise as the importance of the subject warrants. In other endeavors that are relevant to Amer-ica's competitiveness, such as research on the burdens of regula-tion, the training of school principals, or the development of scholars in international subjects, government funding has tended to be scanty, shifting, and unpredictable. As a result, universities have had difficulty attracting first-rate faculty to work in these fields.

Money aside, the nation also lacks a forum in which public officials and university representatives can discuss higher educa-tion as a national resource and search for more effective ways to respond to national problems through research and advanced education. In some states, political leaders and university presi-dents do talk periodically in an effort to link higher education more effectively to public needs. More often than not, these conversations seem to be useful. But at the federal level, the government is too fragmented to consider how universities relate to national needs in any systematic way. Even if this were not the case, university leaders would be ambivalent about such a dialogue, fearing that comprehensive discussions might eventually lead to detailed planning of a distasteful kind. As a result, such dialogue as does exist takes the form of lobbying by countless associations from higher education with countless federal agencies and legislative staffs. The discussions that result are much too self-serving and dispersed to result in coherent policies and priorities that could encourage universities to respond effectively to the full agenda of national needs.

Because of the way in which our government is organized, it is probably too much to expect that universities and public officials will ever enter into serious, comprehensive discussions over higher education's contributions to the entire national agenda. But it is not too much to hope that government and academic officials could sit down together to consider how universities could respond to individual national issues, such as the efforts that education schools could make to train school principals or the programs that business schools might offer to address problems of production, technology, and design. With only a little effort and funding, such discussions could improve the contributions of universities to a number of important social needs.

It is surprising how little has been said about these contributions in the public commentary about higher education during the past decade. There has been no dearth of criticism regarding the vicissitudes of general education, the neglect of undergraduate teaching, the abuses of intercollegiate athletics, and the yearly surge in college tuitions. Yet no such outcry has occurred over the lack of strong schools of education and public administration or the failure to mount impressive research programs to increase our understanding of poverty, chronic unemployment, homelessness, or the virulent drug epidemic.

All things considered, then, in the constant interplay between universities and the outside world, neither side has done a satisfactory job of promoting the nation's long-term interests. University leaders have not worked sufficiently hard to bring their institutions to attend to our most important national problems. At the same time, neither trustees, nor the professions, nor foundation officers, nor public officials, nor anyone else concerned with higher education has done enough to urge universities to make greater efforts along these lines or to help them mobilize resources sufficient for the task.

There is good reason now to contemplate a fresh attempt to improve on this record. As a new century approaches, and world events promise to leave us less preoccupied with the global struggle between communism and democracy, we are likely to give greater attention to our own society and consider how far we have come in meeting the needs and aspirations of the people. Examining the evidence, we are bound to see with increasing clarity just how serious many of our social and economic problems have become in comparison with the record of other highly developed, democratic societies.

America's problems are sufficiently interrelated that we will be hard-pressed to overcome any of them without attacking them all. And because they are so important and weigh increasingly on the lives of every citizen, it is virtually certain that we will resolve, sooner or later, to make a sustained commitment to address the entire agenda on a scale commensurate with the interests at stake.

Once such an enterprise is launched, the question will arise whether the nation can command the knowledge and the trained personnel it must have in order to crown the effort with success. At this point, the contributions of our universities will prove decisive. As matters now stand, however, their ability to meet the challenge is very much in doubt. Although the potential

exists to respond to almost every issue on our formidable national agenda, the readiness to do so does not. As we have seen,
most universities continue to do their least impressive work on
the very subjects where society's need for greater knowledge and
better education is most acute.

It is tempting to ignore such shortcomings at a time like the
present when the willingness throughout America to confront
our urgent problems seems so small in relation to the need. But it
is precisely in such times that universities must respond so that
they will be ready to make their full contribution when the nation
turns its attention again to the broad agenda of reform. The work
of the academy will not bear fruit overnight. We will need years
to develop the educational programs and to make the discoveries
and advances that will help society to progress. Hence, it is
important to begin and not to temporize or defer to other more
immediate reforms. In this, we can recall the story President
Kennedy used to tell about Marshal Lyautey after he assumed
control of France's territories in North Africa. Surveying the
barren countryside around him, he remarked to his aide, "We
must plant trees." "But sir," the aide responded, "in this environment, it will take one hundred years for a tree to grow to its
full height." "In that case," Lyautey replied, "we have no time to
lose. We must begin this afternoon."

NOTES

Introduction

1 William B. Johnston, *Workforce 2000: Work and Workers in the Twenty-First Century* (Indianapolis, Ind.: Hudson Institute, 1987).

2 Colin Norman, "Rethinking Technology's Role in Economic Change," *Science* (May 20, 1988): 977.

3 The *Asian Wall Street Journal,* May 5, 1986.

4 See, e.g., International Association for the Evaluation of Educational Achievement, *Science Achievement in Seventeen Countries* (New York: Pergamon Books, 1988); Archie Lapointe, Nancy Mead, and Gary Phillips, *A World of Difference: An International Assessment of Mathematics and Science* (Princeton, N.J.: Educational Testing Service, 1989).

5 Wilfred Cantwell Smith, review article, *Dalhousie Review* 57 (1977): 540, 546.

6 Timothy Fuller, ed., *The Voice of Liberal Learning: Michael Oakeshott on Education* (New Haven, Conn.: Yale University Press, 1989), p. 41.

Chapter 1

1 Harvey Brooks, *The Research University: Centerpiece of Science Policy?* College of Business, Working Paper Series 86-120 (1986), pp. 7–8.

2 Richard Cyert, Statement before the House of Representatives Committee on Commerce, Science and Technology (mimeo) (1987), p. 8.

3 Erich Bloch, *Basic Research: The Key to Economic Competitiveness* (National Science Foundation, 1986), p. 12.

4 Erich Bloch, Testimony before the Subcommittee on Science, Technology and Space, Senate Committee on Commerce, Science and Transportation, September 29, 1989.

5 *A Renewed Partnership*, Report of the White House Science Council (1986), p. 3.
6 Quoted in "Japan Is Buying Its Way into U.S. University Labs," *Businessweek*, September 24, 1984, p. 75.
7 Michael Schrage, "Why Subsidize Importers?" *Washington Post*, June 1, 1986, p. C5.
8 See chapters by David Teece and Henry Ergas in Bruce R. Guile and Harvey Brooks, eds., *Technology and Global Industry* (Washington, D.C.: National Academy Press, 1987), pp. 65, 191.
9 Stephen S. Cohen and John Zysma, "Manufacturing Innovation and American Industrial Competitiveness," *Science* 239 (March 4, 1988): 1110.
10 Report: International Association for the Evaluation of Educational Achievement (1988).
11 Curtis C. McKnight et al., *The Underachieving Curriculum: Assessing U.S. School Mathematics from an International Perspective* (Champaign, Ill.: Stipes, 1987).
12 Linda Darling-Hammond, *Beyond the Commission Reports: The Coming Crisis in Teaching* (Santa Monica, Calif.: RAND Corporation, 1984).
13 John A. Dossey et al., *The Mathematics Report Card: Are We Measuring Up?* (Princeton, N.J.: Educational Testing Service, 1988), p. 41.
14 *American Excellence in a World Economy* (Report of the Business Roundtable on International Competitiveness, 1987), p. 41.
15 *America's Competitive Challenge: A Report to the President of the United States* (Business-Higher Education Forum, 1983), p. 23.

Chapter 2

1 Richard D. Lambert, *Points of Interest: An Agenda for a National Foundation for International Studies* (New York: Social Sciences Research Council, 1986), p. 131.
2 Ibid., pp. 9–10.
3 Lyman W. Porter and Lawrence E. McKibbin, *Management Education and Development: Drift or Thrust into the 21st Century?* (New York: McGraw-Hill, 1988), p. 311. This book was written by two business school professors and represents the outgrowth of a three-year study commissioned by the American Assembly of Collegiate Schools of Business. It was based on extensive surveys and interviews involving faculty members and business executives.

4 Michael L. Dertouzos, Robert M. Solow, and Richard K. Lester, *Made in America: Regaining the Productive Edge* (Cambridge, Mass.: MIT Press, 1989), p. 78.

5 Walker, "Our Engineering Schools Must Share the Blame for Declining Prosperity," *Chronicle of Higher Education*, Dec. 2, 1987, p. A52.

6 Rosalie L. Tung, "Selection and Training Procedures of U.S., European, and Japanese Multinationals," *California Management Review* 25 (1983): 57.

Chapter 3

1 J. E. Chubb, "Why the Current Wave of School Reform Will Fail," *The Public Interest* 90 (1988): 28.

2 Ibid.

3 *Marital Status and Living Arrangements: March 1988* (U.S. Department of Commerce, 1988), p. 60. More generally, see Steven Mintz and Susan Kellogg, *Domestic Revolutions: A Social History of American Family Life* (New York: Free Press, 1988).

4 *Child Support and Alimony* (U.S. Department of Commerce, 1987), pp. 6–9.

5 Rexford Brown, Reconnecting Youth: The Next Stage of Reform, A Report (Denver: Education Commission of the States, October 1985), p. 17.

6 *The Family,* Report to the White House from the White House Working Group on the Family (1987), p. 2.

7 Donald L. Kanter and Phillip H. Mirvis, *The Cynical Americans: Living and Working in An Age of Discontent and Disillusion* (San Francisco: Jossey-Bass, 1989), especially chapters 4–6, 8–9; Seymour Martin Lipset and William Schneider, *The Confidence Gap: Business, Labor and Government in the Public Mind* (Baltimore: Johns Hopkins University Press, 1987).

8 *Time*, September 11, 1989, p. 54.

9 George Gallup, ed., *Gallup Poll: Public Opinion 1987* (Wilmington, Del.: Scholarly Resources, 1988), p. 128; *Giving and Volunteering in the United States* (Independent Sector, 1988).

10 Virginia A. Hodgkinson and Murray S. Weitzman, *Giving and Volunteering in the United States*, 2d ed. (Washington, D.C.: Independent Sector, 1988).

11 Ibid.

12 See Herbert Stein, ed., *Tax Policy in the Twenty-First Century* (New York: John Wiley & Sons, 1988), pp. 193, 205.

13 See e.g., John S. Baird, Jr., "Current Trends in College Cheating," *Psychology in the Schools* 17 (1980): 515.

14 Alexander W. Astin and Kenneth W. Green, *The American Freshman: Twenty Year Trends, 1966–1985* (Los Angeles: Cooperative Institutional Research Program, University of California, 1987).

15 Ronald P. Sanders, "The Best and the Brightest: Can the Public Service Compete?," unpublished paper prepared for the National Commission on the Public Service (Washington, D.C.: Volcker Commission, 1988), p. 16; U.S. Department of Commerce, Bureau of the Census, *Voting and Registration in the Election of November 1988* (Washington, D.C., February 1989).

16 Quoted in Mary Louise McBee, ed., *New Directions for Higher Education: Rethinking College Responsibilities for Values (No. 31)* (San Francisco: Jossey-Bass, 1980), p. 5.

17 Saul K. Padover, ed., *The Complete Jefferson* (Freeport, N.Y.: Books for Libraries Press, 1943), p. 1098.

18 Quoted in Douglas Sloan, "Harmony, Chaos and Consensus: The American College Curriculum," *Teachers College Record* 73 (2): 248.

19 William L. Phelps, *Autobiography with Letters* (New York: Oxford University Press, 1939), pp. 329–30.

20 *Annual Report of the President of Harvard University, 1840–41* (1842).

21 *Annual Report of the President of Harvard University, 1841–42* (1843).

22 Bernard Bailyn, "Why Kirkland Failed," in Bernard Bailyn et al., *Glimpses of the Harvard Past* (Cambridge, Mass.: Harvard University Press, 1986), p. 25.

23 Quoted in Laurence R. Veysey, *The Emergence of the American University* (Chicago: University of Chicago Press, 1965), p. 33.

24 Quoted in D. H. Meyer, *The Instructed Conscience: The Shaping of the American National Ethic* (Philadelphia: University of Pennsylvania Press, 1975), p. 68.

25 Quoted in Veysey, supra note 23, p. 45.

26 Ephraim Emerton, "Personal Recollections of Charles William Eliot," *Harvard Graduates' Magazine* (1924), p. 349.

27 Meyer, supra note 24, p. 66.

28 Ibid., p. 134.

29 "Problems of Ethics," Encyclopedia of Philosophy, vol. 3 (1967), p. 119.

30 *Report on Some Problems of Personnel in the Faculty of Arts and Sciences* (Cambridge, Mass., 1939), p. 77.

31 Quoted in Hugh Hawkins, *Between Harvard and America: The Educational*

Leadership of Charles W. Eliot (New York: Oxford University Press, 1972), p. 111.

32 *Annual Report of the President of Harvard College, 1871–72* (1873), p. 13.

33 *Report of the Harvard Committee* (1945), p. 72.

34 Ibid., pp. 72–73.

35 Howard R. Bowen, *Investment in Learning: The Individual and Social Value of American Higher Education* (San Francisco: Jossey-Bass, 1977), p. 220.

36 Meyer, supra note 24, pp. 118–19.

37 *Harvard University Gazette*, October 17, 1986, pp. 1, 8.

38 *New York Times*, October 11, 1986, p. A8.

39 Robert T. Hall and John U. Davis, *Moral Education and Practice* (Buffalo, N.Y.: Prometheus Books, 1975), p. 172. The conventional limit on moral education is expressed by Hall and Davis in the following terms: "The line should be drawn between giving young people the skills and abilities to think morally, along with some practical experience in this domain, on the one hand, and aiming at behavioral or attitudinal changes on the other."

40 See Martha Nussbaum, "Aristophanes and Socrates on Learning Practical Wisdom," in Jeffrey Henderson, ed., *Aristophanes: Essays in Interpretation* (New York: Cambridge University Press, 1980), p. 43.

Chapter 4

1 Karl N. Llewellyn, *The Bramble Bush: On Our Law and Its Study* (Dobbs Ferry, N.Y.: Oceana, 1960), p. 116.

2 Robert K. Massie, Jr., "Prophets to Profits," *Manhattan, Inc.* (August 1985), p. 88.

3 See James R. Rest, "Moral Developments in Young Adults," in Robert A. Mines and Karen S. Kitchener, eds., *Adult Cognitive Development: Methods and Models* (New York: Praeger, 1986), p. 92.

4 See Carol Gilligan, "Moral Development," in Arthur W. Chickering and Associates, *The Modern American College* (San Francisco: Jossey-Bass, 1981), p. 155.

5 L. T. Hosmer, "The Other 338: Why a Majority of Our Schools of Business Administration Do Not Offer a Course in Business Ethics," *Journal of Business Ethics* 4 (1985): 17.

6 See generally, Douglas J. Amy, "Why Policy Analysis and Ethics Are Incompatible," *Journal of Policy Analysis and Management* 3 (1984): 573.

7 Ronald M. Pipkin, "Law School Instruction in Professional Respon-

sibility: A Curricular Paradox," *American Bar Foundation Research Journal* (1979): 247–75; see also E. Gordon Gee and Donald W. Jackson, "Current Studies of Legal Education: Findings and Recommendations," *Journal of Legal Education* 32 (1982): 471, 488–94.

Chapter 5

1 Bernard Bailyn et al., *Glimpses of the Harvard Past* (Cambridge, Mass.: Harvard University Press, 1986), p. 131.

2 William John Bennett, *To Reclaim a Legacy: A Report on the Humanities in Higher Education* (Washington, D.C.: National Endowment for the Humanities, 1984), p. 25.

3 National Education Association, *Resolutions, New Business, and Other Actions, 1976–77* (1978), pp. 27–28.

4 Robert A. Gordon and James E. Howell, *Higher Education for Business* (New York: Columbia University Press, 1959); Frank C. Pierson, *The Education of American Businessmen: A Study of University-College Programs in Business Administration* (New York: McGraw-Hill, 1959).

Index

rity, 13, 57; officials, 43, 46, 61, 114; policy, 31, 82; political scandals, 72; politicians, 34; programs, 57, 82, 119; science policy, 11. *See also* Congress, U.S.; Department of Defense, U.S.; Department of Education, U.S.; Military, U.S.; Public officials

Universities: academic environment, 21, 84, 85, 95–98, 103, 111; administration, 85, 90–92, 97, 107, 110, 112, 120; admissions, 32; affirmative action, 90, 91; alumni, 41, 51, 64, 74, 113, 117; athletic teams, 79, 88, 91, 94, 97; careerism in, 8; deans, 52, 69, 90, 97, 107, 109, 110, 113; enrollment, 10, 91; ethics in, 62, 70, 85, 86, 90, 91, 94–95, 106; extracurricular programs, 42, 80, 88, 99, 103; faculty, 10, 38, 41, 69, 70, 74, 86, 90, 95, 96, 107, 109, 111–13, 117; financial aid officers, 94, 97; history, 51, 87, 102; intellectual standards, 8, 9, 22, 52, 77, 95; isolation from society, 5, 47–48, 105, 112; judicial boards, 86, 87; presidents, 14, 52, 63–65, 67, 68, 90, 92, 107, 110–12; priorities, 49–52, 62, 85; provosts, 18, 110; reputation, 3, 4, 50, 51, 69, 91, 111; size, 10, 87; spokesmen, 29; student activism and protests, 9n, 86, 92; student involvement, 86, 87, 89; student organizations, 85, 99; trustees, 111, 115, 121. *See also* Graduate pro-

grams; Professional schools; Undergraduate programs; individual discipline entries; individual graduate and professional school entries; individual university entries

University of Notre Dame, 109

University of Wisconsin, 68

Urban areas: disintegration and decay, 35, 55, 106; ghettoes, 35, 41, 89; growth, 67; revitalization, 7, 89

Volunteers and voluntary organizations, 57, 60. *See also* Community service

Walker, Eric A., 35

Walker, James, 68

War Against Poverty, 35, 40

Washington Post, 3, 18

Wayland, Francis, 63, 66, 67

Welfare programs. *See* Social problems: social welfare; welfare programs

White-collar crime, 59, 72, 73

White House Science Council report, 14

Wilson, Woodrow, 65, 68

Women's issues, 71–72, 89, 95

World War II, 2, 68, 70

Wright, Orville and Wilbur, 2

Yale University, 64

Zanna, Mark P., 84

Derek Bok is president of Harvard University and a professor of
law. Before assuming the presidency in 1971, he was the dean of
Harvard Law School. He has consistently displayed a special interest in education with particular emphasis on programs and curricula that respond to the needs of society and prepare the
individual for life in an increasingly complex and international environment. Mr. Bok is a strong proponent of the teaching of
ethics. He also advocates a broad liberal arts education, improve-
ments in the methods and the quality of teaching, and professional training for public service.

Library of Congress Cataloging-in-Publication Data
Bok, Derek Curtis.
Universities and the future of America/Derek Bok.
ISBN 0-8223-1036-8
1. Education, Higher—Social aspects—United States.
2. Education, Higher—United States—Aims and objectives.
3. Universities and colleges—United States.   4. Moral education
—United States.   I.   Title.
LC191.4.B65   1990
378'.01'0973-dc20   89-49196